# A Mentor's Fingerprint

What we leave for tomorrow starts today.

*[signatures]*
and Donna Inglis

# A Mentor's Fingerprint

Leave a mark. Make a difference.

Ann Griffiths & Donna Inglis

Pleasant Word
A Division of WinePress Group
PW

Pleasant Word (a division of WinePress Publishing, PO Box 428, Enumclaw, WA 98022) functions only as book publisher. As such, the ultimate design, content, editorial accuracy, and views expressed or implied in this work are those of the author.

ISBN 13: 978-1-4141-1474-3
ISBN 10: 1-4141-1474-5
Library of Congress Catalog Card Number: 2009904480

We dedicate this book to those who have patiently mentored us
and to those whom we have had the privilege to mentor.

# Contents

## Section IV: The Skills of Mentoring

## Section V: The Imprint of Mentoring

# Preface

THE JOURNEY FROM concept to completion of this book is one we'd like to share with you, but more importantly we want to emphasize that what you're holding in your hands is not intended to show you how to create another program. Rather, it is meant to awaken the reality that we all mentor every day and to provide you with skills to do it better. We believe that as we all come alongside one another, we are encouraged in our walk with God, and friendships and families are strengthened.

Shortly after Ann and her husband began attending the same church as Donna and her husband, Ann was asked to head up the ministry to women and Donna agreed to be part of the women's leadership team. Though we had previously known each other, we became close friends as we worked together. We also learned that we had a lot in common—including our belief in the importance of mentoring.

As we talked about the value of mentoring we realized that, even though there wasn't a formal mentoring program in our church, mentoring was taking place. However, while women were mentoring women and men were mentoring men as part of their everyday lives, they did not necessarily see themselves as mentors, or realize that they were mentoring. We believed that learning added skills would further enhance the lifestyle mentoring that we saw happening.

To test our belief, we created a rough outline of what we might teach in a weekly course and promoted it to the women of our church to determine their level of interest in the subject. To our delight enough women registered to fill not one, but two classes.

Armed with this confirmation, and a deadline to begin in two weeks, we began developing the course content—keeping one lesson ahead of the class. Each week, we challenged women to use the skills we taught. And each week, we heard enthusiastic reports about the positive effects they were seeing in their life, their work, their ministries, and the people with whom they were in contact.

As the course progressed, we received encouragement to put our material into book form and believed God was leading us to proceed down that road. When a friend recommended a Christian writers' conference that was being held in a nearby city, we decided to attend with two goals in mind: to learn more about publishing, and to confirm that God really was leading us in this direction. At the last moment, we threw our lesson material into the trunk of the car. When we walked into the conference, we knew we were supposed to be there and that God had already set everything in motion for the message of this book to reach many people. We simply had to trust Him and take each step as it came along—even though we didn't know where the path would lead.

Not long into the conference, we met Athena and part of the team from WinePress Publishing. The connection was immediate, as we discussed our vision and heart to see men and women understand the value of mentoring in their everyday relationships and recognize that they too are being mentored. Two days later, we were on our way home from the conference with a confirmed publisher for our book and a huge challenge ahead of us. The lessons now needed to be rewritten and expanded into a publishable manuscript.

This book would not have been possible without the amazing support and willingness of the women who participated in the two classes that launched our original material. It is with love and appreciation for each of you that we thank you for "going with the flow" and giving your insightful feedback. May you continue to influence others and leave a mark for eternity.

Thank you to the WinePress Publishing team: Athena Dean for believing in us and the message of this book; Tammy Hopf and crew for taking care of us and all the details; and our editor/coach Barbara Kois for your brainstorming, editing knowledge, and giving us room to be ourselves so we could grow with your guidance through the process. Our phone conversations and emails have morphed into evolving friendships with each of you.

A special thank you to our husbands, Jim and Max, for your faith in us and for being our special champions. You have always believed in us—for which we are forever grateful. Thank you too to our families and closest friends who cheered us on with, "You can do it."

And a big thank you to you, our reader, for picking this book up, reading it, and encouraging others to do the same. May you be inspired and challenged to put the principles and skills of this book into practice. And may you leave an unforgettable mentor's fingerprint on the world.

—**Ann and Donna**

P.S. from Donna

The book you hold in your hands is the work of Ann, whom I believe to be a gifted writer. I have been blessed to work alongside her as I shared thoughts and experiences and fulfilled research needs. But Ann is the one who has diligently labored over it and made it a reality. May you learn, as we have, that God put us into a body to impact each other for growth and for His glory.

# Introduction

WHEN DONNA AND I were children, life principles were fed into our lives by people who took an interest in us. During our teen and young adult years, men and women encouraged us to discover and sharpen our gifts and talents. They guided us as we maneuvered our way toward adulthood. Even now, there are people we value as our mentors—friends who share their wisdom and experience when we need someone to walk with us through challenges or victories. And yes, we mentor each other.

Before Donna and I committed to co-create and teach our first mentoring course, our conversations were peppered with memories of people who had made an impact on our own lives—people who had mentored us—some intentionally and some unknowingly. Throughout this book, you'll meet some of those men and women.

In turn, we want to help you remember those who left a mark and made a difference in your life. We want you to understand that you are mentoring others as you come alongside them, sharing your experiences and insights. We want you to think about what kind of fingerprint you're leaving on the people in your life. And we want to give you tools to help you be an even more effective formal or informal mentor.

In truth, we all mentor all the time, whether we realize it or not. Those who made a difference in your life may not have thought of it as mentoring. Maybe they were teachers or club leaders who took a special interest in you. Or perhaps it was someone who guided you through a difficult period in your life. Or maybe it was a friend or relative who shaped your attitudes as you watched him or her maneuver a difficult situation or respond to a significant success. Whether they realized it, or you understood it, they were mentoring you.

Mentoring crosses generational, cultural, and economic boundaries. It's where mentors and mentees enfold and engage one another in healthy relationships that encourage growth in all areas and stages of life. It empowers us to live a transformational lifestyle that strengthens us in our relationships and encourages us in our walk with God.

We have seen many come to a newfound freedom as they became more intentional in feeding into the lives of others, and as they implement the skills you will learn in *A Mentor's Fingerprint*. Our desire is that you too will gain that same enthusiasm, and experience what mentoring can do in and through your life as you allow yourself to be used by God to reach into the hearts of people and affect their lives for eternity.

We truly hope that *A Mentor's Fingerprint* will inspire you to leave a mark and make a difference.

# SECTION I

# The Evidence for Mentoring

# CHAPTER 1

# Moments in Time

*There is nothing in a caterpillar that tells you it's going to be a butterfly.*

—R. Buckminster Fuller

THE MORNING SUN warmed my face as I drove through the metal gate and onto the paved parking lot that surrounded a steel and glass office building. It wasn't until I entered my new client's corner office and glanced out the window that I realized I was looking at the land my paternal grandparents had homesteaded in the early 1900s. This was the company that had, years before, transformed my grandparents' hay and alfalfa fields into concrete and asphalt. This was the acreage where my uncle had died at the age of ten, my father was born, and I spent the first six years of my life.

My grandparents' journey to this part of the world began when my grandfather left my grandmother and their two boys in England to build a home in the land of opportunity. When they joined him a year later, they cleared, plowed, planted, and worked hard. They laughed and cried. They won and lost. And they built a home that they dreamed would last for generations.

But the dream ended when this same corporation that now contracted with me to coach a couple of their executives, had expropriated my grandparents' land. When Grandma and Grandpa refused to leave, men with bulldozers and heavy machinery rolled up to the front of the farmhouse to take possession. And my eighty-something, defender-of-justice grandfather met them at the door with a shotgun, in a valiant, but futile, attempt to save his home from corporate progress.

As I drove away from the sprawling glass and steel buildings, I reminisced about early life on the farm and how hard my grandparents had worked. Not only had they been farmers; they had also been courageous pioneers who left indelible fingerprints of their lives on my life.

I let my mind replace the now paved road with the fields that I ran in as a child. I pictured my grandparents' English-style cottage and the home that my father and grandfather had built for my parents when they were married. I saw myself as a young girl walking over the railroad tracks that ran through the middle of the farm, dividing our home from the rest of my grandparents' acres of land. I recalled my white-haired grandma standing at the pole fence and waving as I hiked across the field to get the goat's milk that was the only thing my little sister could drink. And, in my memory, I heard Grandma call to me as my five-year-old legs ran toward her tall frame. I felt her calluses as we walked hand in hand toward the barn. I smelled the damp soil of the root cellar as we descended the stone stairs to pick out some vegetables. And I heard my grandma scold the chickens who disapproved when we entered the coop to gather their eggs.

Now, more than fifty years later, I drove past buildings and street lights. There was nothing to show that my grandparents had ever been there or that once upon a time, my sister and I ran in the fields and picked buttercups. Even the road that once bore my grandparents' name was now a number and the gardens and fields had been replaced with pavement and steel. All that remained was the matter-of-fact recollection of a corporate executive who said, "Oh, yes, this used to be a farm."

Are memories all that remain? True, the farm that my grandparents had developed and the home where I spent the first years of my life are gone. My grandparents are gone, and the family they raised on the farm is gone. What remains are their fingerprints on my life—fingerprints that made a difference. Memories with pictures, words, and feelings all wrapped up in who I am today.

Intentionally and unintentionally, my grandparents mentored me. They taught me by what they said and how they lived. They influenced me by what they achieved and who they were. The life skills I learned, the tenacious spirit I inherited, and the memories I cherish are all part of who I am today. And the journey from generation to generation continues.

When I think about the speck of space I occupy in this world and the tiny role I play in the whole realm of history, I am in awe. On the one hand, I feel irrelevant and wonder what significance I could possibly have on anything. On the other hand, I feel privileged to be part of God's vast creation that stretches from the beginning of time to the end. I am overwhelmed with a sense that I was created to fulfill a special part of God's master plan—for such a time as this.

Maybe you've felt that way too.

Only the passage of time will reveal if something tangible remains to say, "Ann was here" or "Donna was here" or "John was here." However, what I do know is that we make a difference by what we pass on to others through our words and actions.

Our houses may disappear, our books may fade, and our possessions may crumble, but what we leave in the hearts and minds of people will leave an impression on more lives than we will ever know; and we have no idea what beautiful butterfly may emerge.

When we mentor one person, we're not just leaving an imprint on the life of that person. We're also affecting the lives of every person he or she touches.

## For Such a Time as This

The Bible tells us about a man named Mordecai who became the guardian of his young cousin, Esther. After her parents died, he nurtured and guided her into womanhood. As I reflect on that story, I wonder if Mordecai had any idea the impact his mentoring would have. When Esther accepted the challenge to go before the king to defend her people, I wonder if she even thought about the far-reaching implications her actions would have on future generations.

> *Then Mordecai told them to reply to Esther, 'Do not think to yourself that in the king's palace you will escape any more than all the other Jews. For if you keep silent at this time, relief and deliverance will rise for the Jews from another place, but you and your father's house will perish. And who knows whether you have not come to the kingdom for such a time as this?'*
>
> —Est. 4:12-14

God used Mordecai to mentor his cousin Esther and unknowingly prepare her for a special moment in time. Though Esther knew it could cost her her life, she went before the king to plead for the lives of her people.

Esther could have missed out on God's plan and blessing for her life, for her family, and for her people. Instead, she grew into a woman the king chose as his queen and she saved the Jewish nation. If she had turned her back on what she learned from Mentor Mordecai and dismissed the plot to exterminate her people, the

Bible says that God would have raised up someone else to deliver them. And we would be reading a much different story about Esther—if we'd be reading one at all.

Mordecai made a difference in the life of Esther and they both affected the lives of a whole nation, for generations.

What about you? What difference are you making in the lives of people around you? What are you conveying through your words? What are you showing in your actions and attitudes? What mark are you leaving on the lives of your children, grandchildren, and others? Is it an upright and godly example—one that demonstrates the power of God and what He has done in your life? Or do you sometimes find yourself hoping that your children and grandchildren won't duplicate what they see in you?

Think about the difference it could make to future generations if we took time to come alongside a family member. What if we set aside our busy schedule to walk with a friend during a difficult time in life? What if we encouraged a young person to reach beyond his or her comfort zone?

God uses our mistakes, our victories, and ordinary moments to fulfill a greater purpose. We don't know what event or word or action will impact someone. But we do know that we are leaving fingerprints on the lives of people every day. May the moments that make up our lives leave a positive and inspiring legacy.

## Mentoring Moment

1. Think about the family members who have made a difference in your life. What was it about them that influenced you for good or bad?

2. What experiences have given you opportunity to come alongside members of your family?

3. Besides Mordecai and Esther, what biblical family relationships demonstrate a mentoring moment that affected generations?

4. Read at least the first eight chapters of Esther. Which character in this story is your life fingerprint most like: King Xerxes, Queen Vashti, Haman, his wife Zeresh, Mordecai, or Esther?

5. How would you describe the fingerprint you are leaving for your family?

# CHAPTER 2

# Friends for All Time

*Friends are angels who lift us to our feet when our wings
have trouble remembering how to fly.*

—Author Unknown

FRIENDS COME IN all shapes, sizes, colors, and tempera-
ments. They have different interests, talents, and personali-
ties. And they each leave a mark on our lives.

Years ago, it became clear to me that my number one personal
core value is relationships. And it still holds true today. For some
people, this may mean that having many friends around all the
time is important, or that family is everything. For me, the value of
relationships means that I enjoy developing lasting and meaningful
memories in and through loving and close relationships with my
husband, children, grandchildren, and close friends.

Knowing how important friends are to me, my husband, Jim,
daughter, Sarah, and two close friends organized a unique milestone
birthday party for me. To first throw my inquisitive but surprise-
loving senses off, they arranged a dinner for twelve at our favorite

Italian restaurant. It was a relaxed event with lots of laughing, talking, and no one wanting to leave at the end of the evening.

At the dinner party, Sarah gave me a handmade invitation to join her the next weekend for a mother-daughter day. I later learned that it was a setup to get me out of the house while friends arrived and preparations were made for a surprise party.

Sarah and I had a great time visiting antique shops and talking over lunch. I was disappointed when she told me that we had to be home earlier than expected because her husband had a meeting he had to get to. It also turned out to be part of the scheme to "get Mom," because when we arrived home promptly at three o'clock, the house was full of women—all friends of mine, ready to celebrate my birthday.

My dream of bringing girlfriends together from different parts of my life had come true. And here they were—old and new, young and not so young. Friends from diverse cultures and backgrounds with different interests and abilities. Some quiet mannered. Some party lovers. But all classy, strong women with passion and conviction.

It was fun to move from room to room at that party and watch groups of friends chat and exchange stories. These were women of all ages and stages of life, from twenty-something up through eighty-something. Many were meeting each other for the first time and discovering that they like each other. Some had known me for just a few months, others for all or most of my life. Some came from my business and corporate life. Some from my church and ministry life. Some had shared in my music and performance life, and some in my writing and school life. Yet here they were. Each one had made a mark on my life. All had left fingerprints to last forever. New friendships were born and old friends connected at a party that still prompts me to reflect on the diverse friends who have fed into my life—friends who have mentored me.

## Each Friend Makes a Difference

When someone comes into our life, we don't know if the connection will be short-lived or if it will blossom into a lifelong friendship. Sometimes God gives us a special friend to walk with us through a certain phase of our life. Sometimes a friend comes in, goes out, and comes back into our life later on. And sometimes we are privileged to experience a meaningful friendship that lasts a lifetime. Either way, each friend mentors us in his or her own unique way.

As we walk alongside our friends, and they with us, we learn from each other. We encourage each other. We challenge and support each other. When difficult times come, we hold each other close. And when we experience high points, we celebrate each other's accomplishments. In short, our friends mentor us through the good, the bad, and the ugly. And we mentor them.

## Friends Mentor Each Other

One of the most memorable friendships of the Bible is the story of David and Jonathan that begins in 1 Samuel 18. Their first meeting is right after David killed Goliath, who, with the Philistines, had threatened to take the Israelites captive. When David is brought before King Saul and his son, Jonathan, he enters their presence with the bloody head of Goliath in his hand. After David finishes speaking, Scripture says that Jonathan loved David.

> *As soon as he had finished speaking to Saul, the soul of Jonathan was knit to the soul of David, and Jonathan loved him as his own soul.*
> —1 Sam. 18:1

Later in the story of David and Jonathan, Saul and Jonathan are killed in battle and we read of David's lament over their deaths.

*How I weep for you, my brother Jonathan! Oh, how much I loved you!
And your love for me was deep, deeper than the love of women!*
—2 Sam. 1:26, NLT

The biblical example of David and Jonathan teaches us a lot about the everyday things we say and do that serve as mentoring moments between friends. Here are three lessons:

## LOYALTY IS LONG TERM

On more than one occasion, David and Jonathan pledged their loyalty to each other. Beginning with their first meeting and until Jonathan's death, that commitment stayed true.

*Then Jonathan made a covenant with David because he loved him as his own soul. And Jonathan stripped himself of the robe that was on him and gave it to David, and his armor; and even his sword and his bow and his belt.*
—1 Sam. 18:3-4

Loyal friends don't run when the going gets tough. We stand by our friends through life's ups and downs, rights and wrongs.

## ENCOURAGEMENT RENEWS STRENGTH

While King Saul's obsession drove him to pursue David because he wanted to end his life, Jonathan went to David "and strengthened his hand in God" (1 Sam. 23:16). As I read this, I pictured Jonathan taking David's hand and placing it in the hand of God as he encouraged him. During a very difficult time in his life, Jonathan led David to the Source of strength.

When we encourage and pray for each other, we are putting our friend's hands into the hands of God. We are reminding him or her of God's strength in any situation.

**BEING A CHAMPION BRINGS NEW PERSPECTIVE**

Jonathan did more than tell David not to be afraid and that everything would be okay. Jonathan pointed him to the bigger picture. He helped David focus. He told him that Saul would not kill him and that he would be the next king (see 1 Sam. 23:17). He dreamed big for David at a time when David could only see danger around him.

When we come alongside our friends and help them refocus, we help them put circumstances and events into perspective. We cheer them on and we challenge them to reach beyond what they see around them.

## Friends Leave Fingerprints

Do you think of yourself as a mentor to your friends? Conversely, do you think of your friends as mentors to you? Like family members, friends teach and learn from each other. Friends mentor friends through their words and through their actions.

For example, when you pray with, and encourage a friend, you mentor her by guiding her to the Source of all comfort. And when your friend sits and listens while you talk about a concern in your life, she mentors you with affirming words or by asking questions that can lead you to dig deeper or gain a different perspective.

When people look at you and your relationships with your friends, do they see the biblical example of David and Jonathan? Do they see someone they can count on, someone who encourages rather than criticizes, and someone who dreams big when life seems impossible?

Imagine what life would be like if we were all more mindful of the fingerprints we are leaving on the lives of our friends. If we were more aware of how we mentor each other every day, would our actions change? Would our vocabulary change? Would our lives change?

Mentoring as a lifestyle means that we live our lives as if they matter. As if someone is watching, listening, and learning from us all the time. However, it's what's inside us that determines what kind of mentoring example we live and what kind of fingerprint we leave. Later, we will look at the heart and disciplines that set a godly mentor apart from others.

*What you have learned and received and heard and seen in me—*
*practice these things, and the God of peace will be with you.*
—Phil. 4:9

## Mentoring Moment

1. Read the story of David and Jonathan in 1 Samuel 18 to 2 Samuel 1. In addition to the three lessons listed in this chapter, what more can David and Jonathan teach us about how friends mentor friends?

2. Recall a time when you came alongside a friend to challenge, pray, or encourage him or her.

3. What difference would it make in your friendships if you knew that your words and actions were leaving a mark on your friends' lives?

# CHAPTER 3

# Mentoring Matters
—Today

*The wave of the future is coming and there is no fighting it.*
—Anne Morrow Lindbergh

WHEN MY GRANDPARENTS were born in the latter years of the 1800s, the horse and buggy were the primary mode of transportation. In 1928, when my maternal grandmother crossed the Atlantic by ship and traveled by train from Canada's east coast to the west, the trip took close to a month to complete. Almost forty years later, it was a major event for her to take her first plane trip back home to England to visit family and friends. I remember that, to convince herself that air travel was safe, she would say things like, "It doesn't matter if I'm on the ground, on the ocean, or in the air. When my time is up, it's up."

You may recall similar stories from your grandparents. Their generation saw a lot of changes—from horse-drawn carriages to space shuttles, from local skirmishes to two world wars, and from wood stoves to microwaves. And yet, while progress improved their living conditions, the connections they had built as they worked together began to erode. Informal mentoring dwindled as women no longer gathered to create a quilt or can the fruit and vegetables they had grown in their gardens and men no longer came together to harvest their crops or raise a barn.

Then along came the Baby Boomers.

The Baby Boomers are the generation that can name the first family in the neighborhood to get a television set. We know where we were when Neil Armstrong made history as the first man to walk on the moon. We lived through campus riots, anti-war sit-ins, peace rallies, and love-ins. We remember Rosa Parks, Martin Luther King, Jr., and many others who stood for civil rights and against racial discrimination. And we witnessed the election of the first African-American president of the United States.

At school, we learned to type on a heavy, black manual typewriter and scrambled for our turn at the electric one when it was brought into the classroom. Later, at work, we received faxes that took about seven minutes per page to deliver. Today, we can't imagine what it would be like to do business without a computer.

By the time the Gen Xers came along, we found it almost impossible to function without electronics. Cocooning became a trend that drove us further into our own little space and many of us worked from home, content with our phone and computer. As we became more self-sufficient, the face-to-face connection gap widened.

In the past, people talked over the back fence with their neighbors or lingered over a cup of tea or coffee with a friend. Today, those moments take effort on our part as we've become accustomed to instant communication through Facebook®, e-mail, and text messaging—even if we live in the same house. We can only imagine what new communication technologies are on the horizon.

## Today's Reality

My daughter's house is full of electronics. With a husband running his own online business from home, and children who can't seem to live without their computers, iPods, and television, they designated Saturday as a "no electronics day." It's the special day when they read books made with paper and not e-books on their iPods or computers. They play basketball in the backyard and not in the family room with Wii®. They talk without the TV on. And they choose to go to stage plays rather than the movie theater. The first week they tried this, their then ten-year-old son went into electronic withdrawal. But they stayed with it and it proved to be a valuable experience for all of them.

With fast, electronic communication we gain immediate facts and information, but have lost the personal contact that comes when we see a person's eyes and hear the expression in his voice. We know how to text in shorthand but are nervous about talking face-to-face and knee-to-knee. We've become disconnected from close relationships, and though we live in the same house with our family members, we have less time with them. There's an emptiness that needs to be filled—a place where we can feel free to share our feelings and thoughts.

Yes, we live in a world that is very different from that of our grandparents' and parents' generations. Google® has replaced multiple volumes of encyclopedias. Electronic games seem to be replacing board games. E-mail, text messages, and Twitter have replaced handwritten letters and postcards. CDs and iPods have replaced LP (as in long play) records that are foreign to our grandchildren.

Here's a classic. One day my husband and I felt a little nostalgic, so we pulled out our old turntable and a couple of LP records. When our then three-year-old grandson, Anthony, saw what we were doing, he ran upstairs and said, "Mommy, come see the big CDs Grandma and Grandpa have."

In our society's attempt to better understand one another and to grasp the myriad of changes happening in our world, we have differentiated the generations by assigning labels like Silent Generation (born 1930–1945), Baby Boomers (born 1946–1964), Generation X (born 1965–1974), Generation Y or Millenials (born mid 1980s to early 1990s), and Generation Z or the Internet Generation (born mid 1990s through 2000s).

Yet hidden among the generational differences, there are similarities we tend to overlook.

1. We crave the luxury of being still, even for a moment, while a cacophony of sound pollutes our symphony of silence.
2. We ache for someone to walk with us, to teach us, to challenge us, to encourage us, to believe in us.
3. We desire a friend we can trust, a relationship we can depend on, a mentor to guide us, someone to love us for who we are.
4. We long to make a difference.

## Today's Threats

Despite our desire to live significant lives that make a difference, we live fragmented and independent lives in a mobile society that is always changing.

### FRAGMENTED LIVES

We're pulled in multiple directions while we attempt to stay on top of what's going on in our immediate families, let alone remain connected with friends outside our home. We struggle to keep our schedules straight so we can eke out some time and energy for friends and family. Somewhere along the way, we try to squeeze in time for people and activities that we would like to be a part of.

How many times have you tried to get together with a friend whose calendar was as full as yours? Or when was the last time you double-booked yourself because you forgot about something to which you had already committed?

We're caught up in the tyranny of the urgent, and have nothing left to fully enjoy the important people and things in our lives. We're too busy for the intimate relationships we desire. We live fragmented lives.

## INDEPENDENT LIVING

When people learn that my husband and I live in a house with our daughter, son-in-law, and their children, we usually get one of two comments. "I don't know if I could live in the same house as my kids (or parents). How is it . . . really?" or "Wow, I wish I could live that close to my grandchildren. You are so lucky."

Yes, we believe we're blessed to live in a house with three generations. We get to have unexpected conversations about life issues with our grandchildren and they see how Grandma and Grandpa relate to each other on a daily basis. We enjoy impromptu chats with our daughter and her husband as we sit on the stairs that separate our part of the house from theirs or as we visit in each other's sections of the home. We get to bake, garden, and fix things together. We experience lifestyle mentoring in our own home.

In contrast, there are many children who live miles away from their grandparents, aunts, and uncles. In some cases, parents, and grandparents live away from the rest of their family in a rest home or assisted care facility. In these cases, the opportunities for cross-generation learning is limited or non existent.

In the past, as people lived and worked together, boys and girls learned from their parents, grandparents, aunts, uncles, and siblings. And while most of what was passed on had merit, some of what they learned lost its meaning over time.

For example, take the age-old story of the woman who was preparing a roast beef dinner for her family. Her recently married daughter watched as her mom carefully cut a thick slice of good meat off the end of the roast before placing it in the roaster.

"Mom, why did you cut that piece off the end of the roast? It's perfectly good meat."

"Well, that's how my mom cooked her roasts."

When the young bride later asked her grandma why she cut the end off her roasts she replied, "Oh, I did that because the roasts were usually too big for my roaster."

Today, rather than family, young people often turn to other sources for advice and guidance. Generations X, Y, and Z have grown up with Oprah as a spiritual advisor and fashion magazines as their image consultants. Home and Garden TV provides programs to teach us how to decorate on a dime. The Internet has become the go-to reference for learning how to create a special recipe or rebuild an engine.

Our drive for independence has pulled us apart and created surface-type relationships. Families are disconnected. Friends are cautious. Communities are disjointed. When trouble comes our way, or we need to make a major decision, we struggle to think of those to whom we can talk. We long for someone to come alongside us and mentor us.

## MOBILE SOCIETY

According to the National Association of Realtors, people in the United States move to a different home every seven years.[1] While this statistic varies from region to region and country to country, I'm sure that if we included renters, we'd find that people move more often than once every seven years. For instance, during our first ten years of marriage, my husband and I moved twelve times.

There are advantages and disadvantages to living in a mobile society. On the positive side are the range of people we meet, the fun of fresh surroundings and decorating a new home, and the adventure of starting over, to name only a few. However, the challenge is that our mobility and busyness hinders the development of strong and deep relationships. We simply don't take the time to nurture them. And our busyness prevents us from sharing practical day-to-day life lessons or passing on spiritual principles and truths. We don't have time to take time. And we don't take time to spend time. We're always on the move.

## Today's Opportunities

How about you? There are probably people in your life right now with whom you have influence and who would love to spend time with you. It may be someone younger than you in your church or community. It might be a child or grandchild, or a niece or nephew, or a friend's child.

If you think they haven't noticed you, take a closer look. If you think they wouldn't want to spend time with you, think again. In a recent study titled *U@? Communicating with Teens and Young People*, teens said that they "prefer to hang out and talk person to person, but they integrate their communication tactics. Their home phone and Facebook® are their second communication choices if they can't get together personally."[2]

What would happen in our society if we were to embrace mentoring as a lifestyle rather than a program where people have to attend a meeting? How would it affect our world if we became more aware of the impact we have on people in our everyday lives, whether in person or online? What difference would it make if we were to take more notice of what we say and how we act? If we asked ourselves what we need to do differently in order to leave a positive, God-honoring mark?

Whether we have impromptu times with our children or grandchildren or make comments to someone we barely know or handle a delicate situation that involves our friends and peers, we leave a mark. We mentor.

> *Be an example to all believers in what you say, in the way you live, in your love, your faith, and your purity.*
>
> —1 Tim. 4:12, NLT

## Mentoring Moment

1. Recall some changes you've seen in society during your life time. How have these changes affected you?

2. Recount some changes you've seen in the church as a whole within your lifetime. How have these changes affected you?

3. Jesus' mentoring of His disciples changed their attitudes and actions. Identify examples that illustrate the contrast between what Jesus taught His disciples and what they had been taught by the religious leaders of the day. Example: Jesus associating with sinners (Luke 19:1-10).

4. How could mentoring change individual lives today? How could mentoring change our society today?

5. What difference would it make in your life if someone offered to mentor you?

# SECTION II

# The Process of Mentoring

# CHAPTER 4

# Identifying the DNA of Mentoring

*Mentoring is a phenomenon where the past meets the future
in the present.*

—Lindsey Clifford

M Y MATERNAL GRANDMA was the eldest of eight children. She was an independent and adventurous woman who left her family in England to come to Canada to marry a man she had never met. Five years later, my grandfather died and left Grandma with my then four-year-old mother. Sometime during the next eight years, Grandma became a Christian, began attending church, and met my step-grandfather who also lived only five years after they were married. Shortly after his death, I was born.

From the age of two months until I was married, I lived most of my life with Grandma. We developed a special relationship as she mentored me through many situations. Being an encourager with a tenacious and focused pioneer spirit, she was the first to recognize leadership potential in me and prompt me to explore it.

Since that time, my daughter and son have also taken on leadership roles. And as I watch my grandchildren mature, it's a privilege to be part of their growth as they develop their areas of giftedness. What started with my grandma has, to date, left imprints on four generations.

> *One generation shall commend your works to another, and shall declare your mighty acts.*
>
> —Ps. 145:4

How about you? Who left a fingerprint on your life that will make a difference for generations to come?

The bottom line is that mentoring is about relationships. As we dig deeper, we also learn that mentoring can be a formal or informal experience, that it's a journey, and that it's an investment.

## Mentoring Is Formal and Informal

During our lifetime, it's possible to be influenced through formal mentoring and through informal mentoring. Therefore, it's important that we know the difference.

*Formal mentoring* is intentional. It involves a commitment that we make with another person to meet regularly for a designated period of time and for a specific purpose. It flows out of a deliberate desire to learn and grow. And it takes place in a relationship that enables purposeful conversation.

*Informal mentoring* happens when we're affected by what we see in another person's life as we watch him or her from a distance or as we work together. It also takes place when we talk about a problem or explore possibilities and options and come away with an "aha" moment.

## Mentoring Is a Journey

Sometimes mentoring involves a relationship with a mentor that lasts only a short time and for a specific purpose. Other times, a mentoring relationship lasts for years and takes on new dimensions—even to the point of the mentor becoming the mentee and the mentee becoming the mentor.

For the past two summers, I have had the privilege of spending time with Marilyn who is in her late eighties. She is a woman who oozes the spirit of a mentor and began mentoring my friend, Donna Inglis, more than fifty years ago. When Donna took me on a road trip to meet Marilyn, I felt honored and was taken by the genuine love Marilyn had for Donna whom she still greets with open arms and a warm "Hi, Sweetie." It's a beautiful picture of a daughter coming home to her mother.

Their relationship began when Donna was barely a teenager and Marilyn became her Sunday school teacher. As Marilyn taught scriptural truths with life application, Donna's thirst to grow in her walk with God kept her coming back for more. They spent hours in conversation, either around Marilyn's dining room table, or on long walks, or as Marilyn worked at her sewing machine. As the relationship grew, Marilyn took Donna to her special prayer place where they'd sit on a rock or a stump by the creek, under the evergreens to talk and to pray.

As she reflects on those early days, Donna remembers Marilyn as being very serious about her relationship with the Lord and about life in general. Donna, on the other hand, was a prankster who was usually up to mischief.

From time to time, her knack for teasing could no longer be contained, so she'd torment Marilyn by doing things like holding doors so she couldn't get out of the bathroom or upstairs. Through it all, Marilyn accepted Donna's high-spirited playfulness with a smile.

When it came time to leave for Bible school, Marilyn, who was a seamstress, sewed clothes and also made everything that was needed for Donna's dorm room. Years later, at graduation, Donna's mom and several others from the church traveled north to Three Hills, Alberta, Canada to see her graduate. Marilyn, who was part of the group, arrived with a dress box containing a dress that she had specially made for the occasion. But there was a problem.

Marilyn explained that when she measured the finished dress, it fell short of the regulation length required by the school. So, to correct the mistake, she confessed that she had added white lace around the bottom of the dress. Donna recounts that, "My face must have turned pale. But as Marilyn opened the box, my mom and the rest of the women burst through the door laughing." Marilyn had succeeded in getting back at Donna for all the years of taunting and teasing. The dress was perfect. And there was no lace.

When God led Donna to Trinidad as a missionary, Marilyn gave financially from what she earned as a seamstress, provided a place for Donna to live when it was needed, sewed clothes for her, prayed constantly, and supported her in any practical way she could. Donna even left her aging parents in the capable and loving hands of Marilyn who had become like a daughter to them.

In her book, *Between Women of God,* author Donna Otto, talks about "daughters of the heart"[3] which is the kind of relationship Donna feels with Marilyn. Together they have journeyed over rocky roads and happy trails. Marilyn has mentored as counselor, teacher, coach, and spiritual guide. And, yes, at times the mentor has been the mentee and the mentee has been the mentor. But, to this day, Donna gratefully and affectionately refers to Marilyn as her "mother of the heart."

When we begin a mentoring relationship we don't know how long it may last. It could be a short jaunt or a long voyage. Either way, it is a journey to be cherished as a friendship with purpose.

## Mentoring Is an Investment

In her mentoring program, Ann Rolfe defines mentoring as "an alliance that creates a space for dialogue that results in reflection, action, and learning."[4]

This alliance, I believe, is a commitment between two people who are making a mutual investment. It's a safe relationship where honest conversation takes place and where "reflection, action, and learning" result in valuable returns.

When we, as mentors, invest our time, our knowledge, and our energy into another person, we are saying that she matters. We care about her dreams and aspirations. We care about her frustrations and heartaches. We care about what makes her happy and sad. We care about her.

The longer I live, the more aware I am about the value of this mentoring investment. The more conscious I am about the individuals who have invested in me, and the more attentive I am about how I am investing in others.

As I look at my family, the concept of lifestyle mentoring and the fingerprint I'm leaving really hits home. As much as I love the relationships I have with other people, it's when I look at my children and grandchildren that I can't get away from the reality that I'm investing in the next generation and the next and the next. It has become important to me and I realize that a mentoring commitment today is an investment for eternity. It's never ending.

Whether formally or informally and whether we're living our lives in front of our family or before those we don't even know are watching, mentoring is an investment that pays high eternal dividends that we will never fully comprehend.

# What Mentoring Is Not

If you jumped to this section to see what mentoring is not, you've missed a very important lesson. I believe that when we first know what something is, it's easier to identify the "is not."

For example, when someone is trained to detect phony money, he is not given counterfeit bills to study. He is given real money. He learns what the genuine item looks like and feels like. He becomes so familiar with it that he can instantly spot a counterfeit bill when it's given to him.

So—if you haven't yet studied the real thing, go back to the beginning of this chapter and read what mentoring is. Go ahead. Donna and I will wait right here for you.

Okay, now that you've read what mentoring is, the mentoring "is not" will be clearer to you. Here is a chart that lists a few "is" and "is not" descriptions. Before you read beyond this chapter, I suggest that you become familiar with these entries and check the references provided beside them.

**Illustration 1—Identifying the Real Thing**

| Mentoring IS NOT... | Mentoring IS... | Scripture says... |
| --- | --- | --- |
| Taking responsibility for what another person chooses to do or not do | A God-commanded responsibility to pass on wisdom and practical skills | Titus 2:2-6 |
| A place to share juicy bits of gossip | A safe place where privacy is respected and confidences are kept | Proverbs 11:13 |
| Selfish | Selfless or self giving | John 15:13 |

| Focusing on the mentor | Focusing on the mentee | Acts 18:24-26 |
|---|---|---|
| Being judgmental | Supportive | Ecclesiastes 4:9 |
| Meant to encourage self-sufficiency from God | Intended to encourage dependence on God | Malachi 3:14-16 |
| Being an expert in everything | Sharing appropriate and timely information | Daniel 1:3-4 |
| Ego building for either the mentor or mentee | A gift that is shared | Matthew 22:39 |
| Devaluing or putting someone down | For development of the mentee | Proverbs 27:17 |
| Making decisions for the mentee | Empowering the mentee | 1 Samuel 25:1-35 |
| A hat you put on and take off | A lifestyle | Titus 2:7-8 |

## Evolution of Mentoring

In Homer's epic poem, *Odyssey*, Mentor was the son of Alcumus who, in his old age, became the trusted friend of King Odysseus. When the king left for the Trojan War, he placed Mentor in charge of his household affairs and of his son, Telemachus. For years, Mentor trained Telemachus in all the ways a father would equip a son for life.

The first recorded modern usage of the word "mentor" is in a book titled *Les Aventures de Telemaque* by Francois Fénelon, in which the lead character is named Mentor. Published in 1699, it was widely read in the 18th century.[5]

Throughout time, many of the world's most successful people have benefited from having a mentor. In music, Johann Christian Bach mentored Wolfgang Amadeus Mozart. In sports, five-time Tour de France winner Eddy Merckx mentored Lance Armstrong who went on to win the same title seven times. Aristotle mentored Alexander the Great, and on we could go across occupations and ages.

Mentoring crosses generational, cultural, and economic boundaries. It takes place when mentors and mentees enfold and engage one another in healthy relationships so as to encourage growth in all areas and stages of life. It empowers us to grow as individuals, strengthens us in our relationships, and encourages us in our walk with God. Add to that, the premise of this book, which says that mentoring is a lifestyle, and we are 24/7 mentors.

Mentoring takes place all the time because we all mentor and we are all mentored everyday. Without being conceited or arrogant, our words and actions are affecting other people all the time. Our life is on display. The key, however, is that it is our choice what kind of life we live; what kind of fingerprint we leave.

## Forms of Mentoring

If we asked a group of individuals, "Who has mentored you in your lifetime?" most would tell us about a teacher who made a difference in their lives by how they lived and taught them. Or they would recall a coach who motivated them to improve their skills so that they excelled and achieved a particular dream. Teachers and coaches are often seen as mentors, as are counselors and spiritual guides.

In their book, *Connecting*, Paul Stanley and Robert Clinton discuss in detail the major mentoring types and functions. For our purposes, we have highlighted four: counselor, coach, teacher, and spiritual guide.[6] There are professionals who work as counselors, coaches, teachers, and spiritual guides and each has specific training that qualifies them to fulfill unique functions. However, while you may not be trained as one of these professionals, you could, as a mentor, be called on to fulfill a similar role.

As defined in the following chart, you may be asked to give advice or counsel to a friend, to teach from a specific well of knowledge, to coach or motivate someone toward a desired goal, or to guide and direct a mentee in his or her spiritual growth.

**Illustration 2—Select Forms of Mentoring**

| Counselor | Gives timely advice on self, others, and circumstances |
| Coach | Provides motivation, skills, and applications for meeting a task, challenge, or reaching a goal |
| Teacher | Imparts knowledge and understanding of a particular subject |
| Spiritual Guide | Provides accountability, direction, and insight for questions, commitments, and decisions affecting spirituality and maturity |

## What Scripture Says

The terms "mentor" or "mentoring" are not used in the Bible. However, numerous examples illustrate the principles that mentoring is built on. In addition to historical and personal models of mentoring, biblical characters like Barnabas, who mentored Paul, and Paul, who mentored Timothy and Titus, could be called mentors. Ruth, who followed Naomi, and Aquila and Priscilla, who taught Apollos could also be considered mentors.

When we read about the journeys of Paul, it's very clear that his time with fellow believers was spent mentoring them—helping them to grow into a personal and collective maturity in Christ.

If that were not true, he would never have been able to say with confidence what he said to the Philippians and the Corinthians.

> *What you have learned and received and heard and seen in me—practice these things and the God of peace will be with you.*
>
> —Phil. 4:9

> *Be imitators of me, just as I also am of Christ.*
>
> —1 Cor. 11:1, NASB

Scripture shows us that mentoring crosses and builds from generation to generation. In the book of Titus, mature men and women are instructed to teach the younger. Numerous references in the Old Testament emphasize the value of passing on, from generation to generation, what God has done, so that "their children, who have not known it, may hear and learn to fear the Lord your God . . . " (Deut. 31:13).

> *Only take care, and keep your soul diligently, lest you forget the things that your eyes have seen, and lest they depart from your heart all the days of your life. Make them known to your children and your children's children.*
>
> —Deut. 4:9

> *And these words that I command you today shall be on your heart. You shall teach them diligently to your children, and shall talk of them when you sit in your house, and when you walk by the way, and when you lie down, and when you rise. You shall bind them as a sign on your hand, and they shall be as frontlets between your eyes. You shall write them on the door posts of your house and on your gates.*
>
> —Deut. 6:6-9

*Tell your children of it, and let your children tell their children, and their children to another generation.*

—Joel 1:3

When you pass on what you know to others, they in turn pass it on again. And though it's impossible to calculate how many people will cross your path in your lifetime, it is possible to have a positive influence on the magnificence of who they become. How are you affecting future generations? What mark are you leaving on the lives of those around you?

## Everyone Is and Everyone Does

Mentoring is like a rich tapestry. When we first look at it, we don't see the individual stitches that went into creating the beautiful design. We see the beauty of a finished piece of needlework.

So it is with the imprints we leave on a person's life. They are not always visible, but they are still there. They make up one of the many influences on that person's life and they affect the finished design of who that person becomes.

Mentoring is also like an ever-changing kaleidoscope of color. When we peer into the tiny hole at the end of the tube, we're in awe of the intricate design we see. But without the individual pieces of colored glass coming together, the design in the tube would never form and we would never see a beautiful image.

Now translate that to mentoring. The attitudes we project, the example we live, the message we convey with our words, and the tone of those words, are all pieces of us that come together to make a mark. Good or bad, we influence others just as they influence us. We mentor others just as they mentor us. In short, everyone mentors and everyone is mentored. Everyone leaves a fingerprint. Every mark makes a difference.

## Mentoring Moment

1. As a mentee, how has your life been affected by one or more of these forms of mentoring: counselor, coach, teacher, spiritual guide?

2. As a mentor, what form of mentoring are you most comfortable using?

3. Read the short book of Ruth, with mentoring in mind.

4. Turn back to the "Identifying the Real Thing" chart shown earlier in this chapter and review the list that describes what mentoring is.

5. How is each item in the "mentoring is" column demonstrated in the relationship between Ruth and Naomi?

6. As a mentor, how are you like Naomi in someone's life? As a mentee, how are you like Ruth?

# CHAPTER 5

# Growing Through the Journey

*It takes a deep commitment to change and an even greater commitment to grow.*

—Ralph Ellison

WHEN MY CHILDREN were babies they were totally dependent on their daddy and me. As they grew into their preteens and on through the teenage years, they did what most teenagers do. They pushed boundaries and craved independence.

Now in their thirties, Sarah and James have reached the adult stage of inter-dependence and we are blessed with wonderful relationships. They are still our children, but now we share the added dimension of life with them as inter-dependent adults, learning and growing together.

## Stages of Growth

The stages we watch our children go through—from babies on into adulthood—are very similar to the development that a healthy mentoring relationship experiences. Here's what I mean.

## BABY STAGE

As babies, our children are dependent on us for things like food, shelter, and comfort. In the early stages of a mentoring relationship, mentees can be like children. They look to their mentor for support, encouragement, and a safe place to be.

## TEENAGE STAGE

When our babies grow into their teen years, they push parental boundaries, in their desire for independence. So it is with mentees. As they are encouraged in their growth and in who God created them to be, they gain confidence and begin to step outside their comfort zone.

## ADULT STAGE

Moving into the adult stage of inter-dependence can be a delightful experience for both parent and child. And the same is true for a mentor and mentee. As parents and children learn to interact on a different level, so mentees and mentors grow as peers and enter into a wonderful period of mutually dependent togetherness.

While we wouldn't dream of leaving our babies unattended, mentees also are not to be abandoned, especially if they are new Christians. And just as it isn't healthy to consider our children as babies forever, so it is with our mentees. If we want them to grow into maturity, we can't view them as being stuck in their child or teenage stage forever. We need to stand back so the child can transform into the adult.

The first two of these three stages of growth can be discouraging. For example, you may have a friend or mentee who appears locked into the baby or teenage stage. Just when you think he is making progress on an issue, he falls back. You watch him take steps forward, only to see him slip and need support to keep going. And, yes, it can feel frustrating. However, encouragement and assurance go a long way. And we all need that from time to time.

An attitude of frustration with our mentee can come across as negative and cause him to not ask for help when he most needs it. On the other hand, an attitude of encouragement may spur him on because he feels loved and accepted.

Be patient. Just as our children change, we need to recognize that our mentees will change. They will stretch and learn and grow. And so will we.

Nicole was a young woman in her twenties with whom I met weekly to formally mentor and coach through various aspects of her life. She had an energetic spirit and big dreams. But she wasn't sure how to go about realizing those dreams, or if they were even possible. Over the course of two-and-a-half years together, she accepted challenges that stretched and grew her. She moved forward, fell down, got back up, and went at it again until, at the end of one of our sessions, she wondered if she was ready to stand on her own.

Based on our history together, we agreed to go through a weaning process rather than stop our sessions abruptly. Our once-a-week meetings moved to every other week for about a month, and then we graduated to once a month for a couple more months. After that, Nicole struck out on her own.

Periodically, via e-mail or Facebook®, we'd catch up on what she was doing and how she was implementing the principles she had learned during our time together. It became evident that she was taking hold of her dreams and fulfilling them.

About two years after our last session, she contacted me and we agreed to meet for coffee. What a wonderful experience to sit across the table and hear about Nicole's adventures and the fulfillment of her passion to work with orphans. She had grown far beyond the baby and teenage stages of our early sessions and was now an inter-dependent adult.

Recently, when I sent her a birthday greeting, it again reminded me of our journey together. It was thrilling to know that she was celebrating her thirty-something birthday with orphans in Africa because she was fulfilling the dream that God had planted inside her many years before.

I've related this story to illustrate the importance of guiding mentees through the journey of growth and recognizing that people do not stop growing after we end our sessions with them.

When I met Nicole for coffee, I realized that she wasn't the same person she had once been. She had grown and was still growing. It was a privilege to see what God was doing in her life and who she had become. She was still the same beautiful young woman with a full heart but now she was fulfilling the life God created her to experience.

We do our mentees a disservice if in our thinking we continue to see them the way they may have initially come into the mentoring relationship—fearful, confused, struggling, or rebellious. As mentors, we need to hold our mentees lightly so they can move through the growth stages and become the inter-dependent adults they are capable of becoming. We must see them as God sees them, saved by grace to fulfill a God-given purpose.

## Seasons of Life

Whether we are in a formal or informal mentoring relationship, age may or may not be an issue. Some people want a mentor who is just beyond them in years or experience. Others look for someone much older with a lot more knowledge. It's also possible for an adult to mentor a child, although this must be done with the permission of the parent involved. Let me illustrate.

Donna mentored Beth, who was a single mom having a difficult time with her ten-year-old son and his homework. Kevin faithfully completed his assignments, but would not hand them in. After working with the mother to help her deal with the situation, but seeing no change in Kevin's behavior, Donna asked Beth's permission to have a phone conversation every night with Kevin before he went to bed.

Each night, he told her how things went in school, and in turn, she asked him if he had completed his homework and whether or not he had handed it in. They then read a Bible story and prayed together. This ritual continued for about two years, night in and night out. Eventually, Kevin regularly handed in his work, went on to college and a career, and is now married with his own children.

Kevin's story shows how mentoring is not restricted by generational boundaries. It crosses generations and allows one to mentor at any age and with any age. Whether a much older person comes alongside a younger person, or friends of the same age mentor each other, both can leave a lasting mark and make a powerful difference. Each age and season of life may have its own unique needs and issues, but everyone mentors and everyone is mentored along the way. The question is, what kind of fingerprint is being left.

In his book, *Mentoring Leaders,* Carson Pue describes three life-time development phases, each representing a specific age group and each asking a key question. As you choose whom you will mentor or who you'd like to mentor you, this summary of the phases will give you some tips on understanding each group and season of life.

AGE OF LEARNING—AGES 18 TO 30—WHO AM I?
In this phase we:

1. Welcome perspective, affirmation, and feedback.
2. Need models we can observe safely.
3. Want to understand who we are and how things work.
4. Are dealing with inner life issues.
5. Need accountability.

6. Have fewer external demands on our time than in later stages.
7. Are best helped by having an older mentor (a good guideline is someone who is ten to fifteen years older).

## AGE OF CONTRIBUTION—AGES 30 TO 50—WHAT DO I DO?

In this phase we:

1. Experience more pressure and are busier.
2. Enter a midlife re-evaluation time.
3. May dabble in different things and not make a significant contribution anywhere.
4. May plateau in our growth.
5. Need coaching and direction in this phase.
6. Have a strong desire to figure out our purpose.
7. Are best helped by having a combination of senior and peer mentors.

## AGE OF INVESTMENT—AGES 50 PLUS—IN WHOM OR WHAT SHOULD I INVEST MYSELF?

In this phase we:

1. Will attend more funerals than weddings.
2. Turn our focus to "finishing well."
3. Have a growing desire to leave a legacy—leave a lasting imprint or impact.
4. Can enjoy a vibrant time of growth and learning.
5. Will see a great deal of change (e.g., family dynamics, moving).
6. Are best helped through a peer mentor, one close to our age who will grow old with us.[7]

## Growing Pains

When Jesus walked this earth and mentored His disciples, they too experienced growing pains. One example of this was when they were in the Garden of Gethsemane where Jesus had gone to pray because, as Mark tells us in chapter 14 verse 33, "He began to be greatly distressed and troubled." Jesus knew that He would soon be betrayed and arrested, so He asked Peter, James, and John to keep watch for Him while He went to pray.

> *And He said to them, "My soul is very sorrowful, even to death. Remain here and watch."*
>
> —Mark 14:34

But after He had prayed, "Abba, Father, all things are possible for you. Remove this cup from me. Yet not what I will but what you will" (Mark 14:36), He returned to the three and found them sleeping. In His agony, at a time when He needed support, His mentees became like children and fell asleep.

> *And He came and found them sleeping. And He said to Peter, "Simon, are you asleep? Could you not watch with me one hour?*
>
> —Mark 14:37

I wonder if Jesus felt frustrated with their lack of maturity. Did He feel as if they had taken two steps forward and four back? Did He wonder if they would ever make it without Him? Could He trust that they would stand strong during the events of the coming days?

Each of us goes through stages of growth. And yes, we sometimes revert back to being the child who needs extra support or the teenager who tests the boundaries. I know that I sure do. Yet God in His infinite wisdom tells us to "bear one another's burdens" and to walk alongside each other so that we will go on to maturity.

Imagine what life would be like if we accepted each other where we are in our growth and lived a life that left a fingerprint of encouragement and challenge. What difference would it make to our families? Our churches? Our world?

## Mentoring Moment

1. What season of life are you in right now: the age of learning, age of contribution, or age of investment?

2. What stage of growth are you in right now? Are you in the child, teenager, or adult stage?

3. What is holding you back from moving along in your journey of growth?

4. What do you need to let go of in order to move forward? Share this aspect of your journey with a mentor or friend who can pray with you and hold you accountable if that is your desire.

CHAPTER 6

# Developing the Mentoring Relationship

*There comes that mysterious meeting in life when someone*
*acknowledges who we are and what we can be, igniting the*
*circuits of our highest potential.*

—Rusty Berkus

ONE EVENING BEV, Denise, Jean, and I got together for dinner. We had met only a few weeks before, through a *Growing Women Leaders* workshop series that I had taught. Though we were a relatively new group of friends, we discovered that we had a lot in common. In addition to all of us being in positions of leadership, we shared a passion for ministry and learning, a shared love for people, and a shared commitment to see God work in and through our lives. As we enjoyed our pot-luck meal, we encouraged and challenged one another. We listened and laughed. We revealed pieces of our personal journeys. And we connected.

As the evening progressed, we talked about our families, our work, and the struggles we had dealt with or were working through. We found that we had all experienced victory and pain in our ministries and were either nursing fresh wounds or carrying scars. And in each situation, we had come to the conclusion that we might not understand it all but we knew that God was in control.

Over that three-hour period, we experienced informal mentoring. We were open with one another and, as a result, we were able to affirm one another and end our time praying together with knowledge and sensitivity.

Did we talk about every aspect of our lives? No. Did we establish a good foundation to support one another and be available in the future? You bet.

Another group of friends with whom I share my life also serves as a good example of lifestyle and informal mentoring. Having known each other for years, we affectionately refer to ourselves as the Fab Five. Lillian, Faith, Loriane, Mary, and I have walked with one another through various life seasons, including careers, marriages, births, and deaths. And now retirement and grandchildren issues have crept into our conversations.

When we get together for our regular dinners or weekend getaways, our discussions range from nitty-gritty, day-to-day life matters and our visions for the coming year, to deep and complex theological and philosophical issues. No topic is off limits. We give updates, check accountabilities, and express areas of concern. We pray for one another and trust one another implicitly. In short, we mentor one another.

These two slices of life are great examples of informal, peer-to-peer mentoring and they demonstrate how friends mentor each other. They also show that mentoring relationships can be short-lived or long-term experiences. But while mentoring can be informal, it can also take on a more formal approach, which is important for us to understand and is our focus for this chapter.

As stated in chapter four, formal mentoring is deliberate. It's a commitment made by two people to meet regularly for a specific purpose and period of time.

The following principles apply primarily to the formal mentoring relationship. However, you will find that much of what is covered here is also valuable in more informal relationships.

# PRINCIPLE #1

## Initiating the Mentoring Relationship

A mentoring relationship can be initiated by anyone who would like to be mentored, or by a person who sees need or potential in someone else and offers to mentor him or her. Therefore, we'll look at this initiation phase from both the perspective of the mentor and the mentee.

### THE MENTOR'S PERSPECTIVE

Jesus was intentional when He chose all twelve of His disciples. He was with them for three years, mentoring and preparing them for the future when He would send them out to do what He had taught and lived in front of them.

> *And He went up to the mountain and summoned those whom He Himself wanted, and they came to Him. And He appointed twelve, that they might be with Him, and that He might send them out to preach, and to have authority to cast out the demons.*
> —Mark 3:13-15, NASB

Just as Jesus carefully chose His disciples, so there are considerations for you to keep in mind as you look at whom you will mentor. Here are six insights to guide you.

### Be Honest

If you're considering a formal mentoring relationship, ask yourself how important this activity is in your life right now. Is the idea just a passing whim or fad? Is it something you think people expect you to do? Is it within your gifting? What's influencing you to take on this responsibility? Be honest with yourself about whether or not God wants you to invest your time and energy in formal, one-on-one mentoring relationships.

## Be Intentional

Watch for opportunities to come alongside someone. When you see an individual whom you think God might be leading you to mentor, find ways to have casual conversation before suggesting your mentoring idea. Ask yourself if this seems to be a person who is teachable; if he or she appears to be interested in having a mentor; and if you believe he or she has a degree of respect for you that would cause him or her to consider meeting with you.

## Be Willing

When you agree to mentor someone it means that you are committing to spend time with this person. You are investing in her life. You are walking with her as person to person, not as helper to helpee. You are reaching out to her, not reaching down to her. When you're considering someone as a mentee, ask yourself if you see potential in her and if you could grow to love and believe in her.

## Be Vulnerable

Search your own experiences to find a common ground, an area where you, as a human being, share the feelings and needs of others. When you find that common ground, don't hide your humanness. Instead, use it to step closer to the person you might mentor. And when you come across someone you could formally mentor, ask yourself if you are willing to be open and honest with him and if you are prepared to allow him to be open and honest with you.

## Be Compatible

Working with a mentee with whom you share similar interests gives you deeper understanding and further common ground to work from. However, while it's helpful in building a bridge for the relationship, it isn't essential to a successful mentoring experience. The key is to consider whether or not you can relate to the person and if you would enjoy communicating with him.

## Be in Prayer

This is not a trite statement. It's the first and last thing you need to do. God knows exactly whom you should be mentoring and who needs you as a mentor. Ask Him to lead you to that person. And continue seeking His guidance as you walk through the mentoring relationship.

## THE MENTEE'S PERSPECTIVE

When the disciples chose to leave what was familiar to them and follow Jesus, they didn't know what was ahead. They simply dropped what they were doing and followed Him. As mentees, we don't have to drop everything to shadow our mentor but there are some things to consider when looking for one.

## Be Courageous

Fear can keep us from moving into the freedom that God wants us to enjoy. Approaching someone to mentor you means that you will have to set aside the fear of rejection, or the fear that she won't want to mentor you, or have the time for you. You'll need to set aside any feeling that you might have about being unworthy of another person's time or a presupposition that she might think you're not worth it. God says you are worth it. He has a mentor just for you.

### Be Vulnerable

It isn't easy to humble ourselves and ask for help. But if you want to change in an area and grow into the person God intended you to be, you need to be willing to be vulnerable and approach someone you believe can mentor you. Be willing to ask, "Would you mentor me?" or say, "I need to be mentored in this or that. Will you help me?"

### Be Committed

Mentoring takes time. It's a commitment made by both the mentor and the mentee. If you want to pursue a mentoring relationship, consider whether or not you are able to adjust your schedule to make it work. Ask yourself if this is the right time for you to commit to mentoring or if it's best to wait for another time. Honor the investment that the mentor is putting into you by doing what he requests (e.g., assignments, accountability). If you are not serious about your commitment and progress, it's difficult to expect the mentor to take it seriously.

### Be Compatible

While it's not necessary for the mentor and mentee to share all the same interests, skills, or gifts, it is helpful to choose a mentor with whom you have some common ground. This will help you relate with him and vice versa. It will also enhance the communication between you.

### Be in Prayer

As in the mentor's perspective, this is not a trivial statement. It's the first and last thing you need to do. God knows exactly who the best mentor is for you at this time in your life. Ask Him to lead you to that person and then continue seeking His guidance as you walk through the mentoring relationship.

# PRINCIPLE #2

## Clarifying Expectations of the Mentoring Relationship

The purpose of any mentoring relationship is to experience change or development and to grow. However, without clearly defined expectations, neither the mentor nor the mentee will know if the relationship has resulted in any kind of growth or change. Entering into a formal mentoring relationship without clarifying expectations is a relationship waiting for disaster to happen. The following guidelines will help you in this phase.

### PRELIMINARY RESPONSIBILITIES OF THE MENTEE

Here are some good questions for the mentee to ask before entering into a mentoring relationship. The questions explore issues such as the mentee's area of need, why she wants mentoring, and what outcomes she desires to see from the mentoring. In other words, they are meant to be a self evaluation for the mentee.

### Sample Questions

How could a mentor be of help to you right now?

What area would you like to focus on with a mentor?

What do you expect from a mentoring relationship at this time?

What outcome would you like to see in your life, as a result of mentoring?

What are some of the qualities in a mentor that are important to you?

Have you been in a mentoring relationship before? Explain.

Write a brief statement describing your own personal spiritual journey.

## PRELIMINARY RESPONSIBILITIES OF THE MENTOR

When someone asks you to mentor her, you could give her the same sample questions listed above. It's a good exercise for her to go through on her own before you meet to discuss the potential of a formal mentoring relationship.

When you have your first meeting, the answers to the questions will guide your conversation, help you assess her need, and determine where she is spiritually. Her body language and the information she provides in her answers will help you decide whether or not you want to go ahead with the relationship.

By the end of this first meeting, you may both feel confident that you want to pursue a formal mentoring relationship. If that's the case, you are ready to move into it.

However, in the course of this initial meeting, you may have a sense that this is not a good fit for you and that someone else might be a better mentor for this person at this time. If that happens, it's best to agree to get back to her within a day or two so you have the opportunity to think and pray about it. You may also wish to contact another potential mentor to see if she is available and willing to mentor. However, you should not feel that it's necessary for you to take on the responsibility of finding an alternative. You may, instead, choose to simply ask the mentee if she has someone else she'd like as a mentor, or you could suggest someone she can follow up with on her own.

It takes courage for a person to ask to be mentored. Therefore, if you are not able to do the mentoring because of time restraints or you don't feel it's a fit, take the following steps.

1. Delay committing to the mentoring relationship at that initial meeting.

2. Take a day or two to prayerfully consider if you are correct in what you're sensing.
3. Determine to either:
    a) Not enter into the mentoring relationship at this time.
    b) Contact a possible mentor who might be a better fit, to see if she is available and willing.
    c) Simply have the name and contact information of a possible alternate mentor available for the mentee to follow up with on her own.
4. Contact the potential mentee again. This needs to be in person or on the phone; not by e-mail.
5. Sensitively discuss what you have decided and do the following:
    a) Tell her that you are not available and that it would be good for her to consider someone else at this time.
    b) Ask her if she knows someone else she would like to have mentor her.
    c) If not, you may want to provide the name and contact information of an alternate mentor that you think might be a good fit and encourage her to contact the person.
    d) Let her know that you are genuinely interested in how she makes out in finding a mentor and ask if she would let you know what progress she makes. Or agree that you will touch base to see how she's doing.

In a mentoring relationship, the focus is on the mentee, not the mentor. As much as is appropriate, be real and transparent in the challenges, failures, and successes you face, but remember, it's not about where you've succeeded or what your experiences have been. It's about the mentee.

Sharing pieces of your life that are suitable contributes to building a relationship of trust and mutual encouragement and allows you and the mentee the freedom to be open and honest with each other. But the conversation is to be centered on the mentee's agenda and her needs and not the mentor's needs.

Identifying the place your mentee is in his spiritual life will enable you to meet him where he is in his journey. If he is a new believer, feed him what he needs for his new life in Christ. If your mentee is young in his faith, teach him biblical truths. If he is into the adolescent stage of his walk, show him how to walk in surrender and obedience to the Lord. And if he is mature in his faith, encourage and challenge him as he learns to use his gifts in ministry and in mentoring others.

If your mentee has not made a personal faith commitment, the mentoring relationship is a great place to demonstrate the difference God has made in your life, not by preaching, but by living a genuine, accepting, and caring life. Be patient and encouraging, and develop trust and friendship as you look to God's Word for wisdom.

> *For, though by this time you ought to be teachers, you need someone to teach you again the basic principles of the oracles of God. You need milk, not solid food, for everyone who lives on milk is unskilled in the word of righteousness, since he is a child. But solid food is for the mature, for those who have their powers of discernment trained by constant practice to distinguish good from evil.*
> —Heb. 5:12-14

## Principle #3

### Establishing Guidelines for the Mentoring Relationship

You will alleviate embarrassment or awkward situations by getting off to a good start and having specific issues talked about before a situation comes up. Here are some basic issues to address at the beginning of your mentoring so as to set appropriate boundaries and come to a mutual understanding of your relationship.

## CONFIDENTIALITY

Guard confidentiality. Both the mentor and mentee need to agree that all information shared in their sessions is private, unless permission has been given to share it.

## SCHEDULE

When mentoring is a lifestyle, it's possible to journey with a mentee over a number of years. However, when you initially agree to a formal mentoring relationship it is advisable to set a specific period of time over which you will meet (e.g., three or six months).

Once you've agreed on the duration of this formal relationship, it's important to establish some schedule parameters. First, set a regular time to meet in person or talk on the phone. Second, determine the frequency that you will get together (e.g., weekly, bi-monthly, etc). Third, agree on the length of time you will meet or speak on the phone (e.g., thirty minutes or one hour).

Putting these parameters in place at the beginning of your relationship will take care of any confusion that could come up as to when and where you're meeting. It could also save either of you from becoming frustrated because the other person is late or going longer than you expected.

## TIME

Always honor each other's time as a valuable gift to be respected. This also applies to emails. If you use this means of staying in touch between sessions, establish an understanding that the e-mail will be acknowledged within a specific time frame (e.g., within twenty-four hours). If there's a question that needs more time to answer, it is still a courtesy to let your mentee know that you received the email and when you expect to get back to her on it.

## VENUE

Choose a place where you both feel safe and where the mentee can speak freely. If you meet in a coffee shop be sure to pick one where there will not be people sitting right next to you. Also, if you have a voice that carries, be mindful of your volume and learn to lower it.

If you are in a public place, or even in a home, and someone approaches one of you, be sure to stop what you're talking about right away. Don't even finish the sentence. You can pick it up after you've acknowledged the person who has interrupted you and he or she has left.

If someone asks to join you, find a polite way to discourage it. You may simply say that you're having a special meeting and that you could get together for coffee with the person another time.

## EXPENSES

If you meet at a coffee shop or restaurant, it's best if you agree at the beginning of your relationship that you will each pay your own bill. By doing this, you won't fall into the trap of wondering who paid last or the feeling of who owes what to whom.

There have been times when I've met with someone in a coffee shop, shortly after lunch. She wanted to order something to eat but I had already had my lunch and only wanted a coffee. She paid for her lunch and I paid for my coffee.

## ACCOUNTABILITY

At the end of a session, you may wish to give your mentee an assignment to help him work on an area that you talked about together. When you do this, there is an expectation that the mentee will be accountable to follow through. However, it is important that your mentee agree to what is being asked and to the level of accountability for completing the homework. If he is not ready to accept it, be open to negotiate on what he is prepared to do, so as to move him forward at a pace he can handle. This is where discernment comes in. Sometimes he may feel apprehensive and simply need a little encouragement. And sometimes he really isn't ready to take as big a step as you think he is.

By establishing boundaries ahead of time, you will know how far to take the person. For example, at the first session with a mentee or coaching client, I have personally made it a habit to ask, "How close do you want me to hold your feet to the fire, when it comes to accountability?"

It may be that your mentee is under a lot of pressure as he comes into the mentoring relationship. He doesn't feel he can possibly cope with being held firmly accountable to something he might not be able to fulfill. In that case, if you were to push too hard, you would be setting him up for failure. However, he may also be the kind of person who wants you to hold him very accountable for what he commits to. Either way, accountability will not be effective in a way that benefits the mentee if he does not first agree to it.

How you word an assignment and the accountability for completing it is also important. Use words and phrases that the mentee has used in your discussion on the issue. This will help him feel more ownership of the homework and better understand the rationale behind it.

One more thing. Do not mistakenly set up accountability that could turn your relationship into a legalistic, performance-based relationship where you become an authoritarian figure that the mentee comes to fear or thinks he must measure up to.

## PRINCIPLE #4

## Identifying Check Points in the Mentoring Relationship

It's important to evaluate whether or not you're on target for achieving what the mentee initially said she wanted to see happen as a result of the mentoring. Check points give both of you the opportunity to adjust the focus or direction if this becomes necessary.

For example, if you have agreed on a three-month, formal mentoring period, it's good to do an evaluation halfway into the three months. This can be done simply by asking a question such as, "Are your expectations being met?" or "What have you taken away from the mentoring so far?" You will also want to ask, "What could we do differently to make the mentoring sessions more effective, if anything?"

## PRINCIPLE #5

## Bringing Closure to the Mentoring Relationship

Finishing well doesn't necessarily mean completion or finality. Rather, it could be that a phase has closed for now and it's simply time for a break. It may be that some breathing space is needed so that what has been gleaned from the mentoring can be absorbed and further applied.

Closure also does not mean that we say, "We've done it. Now we can move on with life and not think about mentoring anymore." You may also find that after an agreed break time, you both want to resume the formal mentoring. On the other hand, you may agree that a mentor with different life skills or experiences is better qualified to facilitate the next phase of the mentee's growth. These are all issues for you to discuss together.

Do not be discouraged if you feel that what you anticipated for your mentee didn't transpire. Remember. It's about him or her, not you. And don't be disheartened if the expectations that your mentee had for herself did not happen. Often, other issues come up along the way that require attention before the mentee can fully work on the expectations he or she initially came with.

As you complete a mentoring period, encourage your mentee to celebrate what he or she achieved throughout the mentoring sessions, regardless of the size of the achievements. Here are two questions to discuss at the close of any given formal mentoring period, so as to determine next steps.

1. What are you taking away from this mentoring period?
2. Now that we're at the end of this mentoring period, what would best help you to continue growing?

## Mentoring Moment

1. Recall a formal mentoring relationship you have entered into in the past. What did you gain from that relationship, either as a mentor or mentee?

2. How does knowing the five principles, outlined in this chapter, benefit you in your formal mentoring relationships? In your informal mentoring relationships?

3. Identify a specific area from Principle #3 that you need to improve on personally.

4. How will you be accountable to achieve this?

# CHAPTER 7

# Avoiding the Barriers to a Healthy Mentoring Relationship

*If we don't create boundaries, we'll create barriers.*
—Author Unknown

THE INCESSANT RINGING of the doorbell jolted us from the deep sleep we were enjoying in our warm beds. Outside, two men stood at the door dressed in bright yellow outfits with bold black letters on their jackets that read "SR"—Search and Rescue.

What could they possibly want with us? We didn't live in a war zone or an area threatened by disaster. We lived in a quiet neighborhood in Abbotsford. But these men looked serious and their voices were urgent when we opened the door.

"If you have kids, grab them and get out now!" they ordered. "We're evacuating the area. A tanker truck has flipped at the gas station, is leaking fuel, and could explode at any moment."

You may never have experienced this kind of emergency but you've likely faced decisions that affect your life. Just when you thought everything was running smoothly, interruptions and unexpected events pulled you away from carefully-made plans.

How would you react? What would you grab, besides your family? What thoughts would run through your mind as you threw on some clothes and ran out the door?

Through the forced evacuation, I was reminded that I have a choice in how I approach unexpected change. That sometimes I may need to anticipate, while other times I may need to adapt. There may even be situations when it's necessary to do both—anticipate and adapt.

Four days before our evacuation, my girlfriend Bev and I were talking about Hurricane Katrina and the devastation it had caused in New Orleans and Louisiana. We pondered how we would react if we had to leave our home immediately and what we would take, if we could take anything.

*That's anticipating.*

On that unexpected morning, the first things that came to mind from Bev's and my conversation was my then sixteen-year-old cat, my laptop computer, my Bible, my reading glasses, and my day planner which held everything including my identification and cell phone.

Once our family had temporarily settled at a coffee shop with other evacuees, we looked over what each of us had grabbed on the way out the door and talked about what to do next. Some of our plans for the day suddenly weren't a priority anymore, but I did have an important conference call scheduled with some of my coaching clients. Given the circumstances, I wasn't excited about finding a corner away from my family to call clients and talk about business issues when my world was uncertain.

However, when the time came, I retrieved the phone number from an e-mail on my laptop, found a piece of paper to write on, buried myself in a semi-quiet corner of the restaurant, and called on my cell phone, which thankfully was charged up.

*That's adapting.*

The same is true in every mentoring relationship. We anticipate and we adapt. Planning well means that we anticipate the possibility of change, while being open and adaptable to change requires that we have a go-with-the-flow attitude. This contributes to the growth of our mentees and the health of our mentoring relationships.

However, no matter how well you plan, the unexpected can happen. In that case, it's up to you whether you choose to see it as an interruption, an inconvenience, an opportunity, or an adventure in the making. If you don't anticipate how you'll deal with changes in circumstances or adapt to changes when they occur, barriers will develop in your mentoring relationship.

## Core Issues that Create Barriers

To identify some of the core issues that create barriers to healthy mentoring relationships, it's helpful to divide them into situational and relational issues.

Situational issues are defined as those that involve the environment or circumstances surrounding a specific concern. Relational issues are those that involve the relationship of people and their interaction with each other.

Whether situational or relational, it's what we do with each issue that determines if a mentoring relationship will be affected positively or negatively. Therefore, as we look at certain issues here, we've tried to point out a potential opportunity or positive outcome as well as a hindrance or negative outcome that could occur.

### SITUATIONAL ISSUES
The situational issues we've chosen to address are: circumstances, flexibility, and freedom.

## Situational Issue #1: Circumstances

From time to time, we all face circumstances that demand a change to our schedule, or a change as to how much we're available, or a change as to how we function because of health or family concerns. Change affects all relationships, even in mentoring.

However, while some of us may thrive on change and see adventure in it, others may fear it or see it as an inconvenience, or vice versa. Either way, change affects some people more than others, and it isn't always easy to manage regardless of perspective.

As we live a lifestyle of mentoring, we need to anticipate and be willing to adapt rather than have a rigid attitude that thinks everything has to stay the same. And remember, some of us may not do well with change.

## Situational Issue #2: Flexibility

It's the responsibility of both the mentor and the mentee to fulfill their commitment to each other and to the mentoring relationship. However, there are times when flexibility is required. Here are some situations that may come up for you and/or your mentee.

### Flexibility is needed when life changes take place

It is possible to enter into a mentoring relationship and later discover that you're too busy or something else has happened in your life to make it impossible for you to continue. How you handle this situation has the potential to grow your relationship or create a barrier. Above all, be honest with your mentee. Let her know if you're in an "I can't do this" or "I can't do this now" situation. Work with her to come up with a solution that accommodates both of you.

*Flexibility is needed when cancellations are made*

Being flexible when a session needs to be canceled is also important. However, be sure to guard against this becoming a regular occurrence. If cancellations become a habit, one of you may begin to feel redundant and your relationship will be jeopardized. As a mentor, if you cancel sessions, a mentee could misinterpret it and think it has something to do with her personally. Or she could think you are too busy for her. Either way, regular cancellations do not help develop relationships of honesty and trust.

*Flexibility is needed when time runs out*

It seems an oxymoron to use the words "discipline" and "flexible" in the same sentence. But when it comes to time, flexibility and discipline go hand in hand.

When you agree on forty-five-minute sessions, do not spend two hours. If you go over on your time once in a while, you must both be in agreement. For example, when I do phone mentoring, I make sure that our thirty-minute sessions are thirty minutes. If we come close to the end of our time and are heavy into a subject, I may bring it to a close by suggesting a bit of homework that will enable my mentee to explore the subject on her own over the coming week. Or I may interject that we only have a couple minutes left, but that I have a few minutes before my next commitment, if she wishes to continue for a bit.

*Flexibility is needed when focus takes a detour*

Another area that may require flexibility relates to the art of staying on subject during a session. For example, if your mentee talks around a subject, or takes little bunny trails into other topics, or babbles on and on about something that doesn't get to the real issue, a lot of time can be taken away from what she really wants to talk about in that session. This will become frustrating to both of you, especially if it happens often.

As the mentor, it's up to you to help your mentee stay on track. Yes, it's okay to have some surface talk and, at times, the little rabbit trails will uncover real issues that are being suppressed. But this will only become evident if you listen. That's the key. You must listen carefully and help your mentee focus.

Getting off focus is not exclusive to mentees. Mentors have also been known to get lost in what they're trying to say. If you are undisciplined in getting to the point, the danger is that you will be drawn into your own agenda rather than your mentee's agenda. And that is a major no-no.

### Flexibility is needed when life happens

Flexibility requires sensitivity to where the mentee is emotionally in any given session. You and your mentee may have agreed that you were going to address a certain issue at your next session. But when you came together, you learned that she had just been devastated by a tragedy or something had seriously impacted her that week. Be sensitive. Be flexible. Use each life situation as an opportunity to help your mentee grow but remember that, sometimes, being a friend with a listening ear is all that's needed.

### Situational Issue #3: Freedom

A healthy mentoring relationship is one that gives both the mentee and mentor the freedom to be who they are and be where they are in their life journeys. But it may require the use of the word "no" from time to time.

Saying "no" is part of setting personal boundaries. And boundaries are healthy for you and for others in your life. The hard part is that some of us seem to need permission to set those boundaries. So if that's what you're looking for, here you go. It's okay to say "no."

I've found that when I say no to someone I'm mentoring or coaching, it models a useful skill for her. It's almost as if she now has permission because she sees me doing it. That said, however, it is important how we say no. And it's important that it not become a habit or something we do because it's convenient. We don't want to come across as someone who doesn't meet commitments or who backs out of something because it's easier than following through.

When you have to say no, try to look at it from your mentee's perspective as well as your own. Think carefully about the alternatives. For example, it may be that you're saying no to a request because you're not available. If so, ask yourself if you could be available at another time and tell your mentee something like, "That would be great. I'd love to do that but it's a bad time for me. Could we do it later today? Or is there another time this week?"

Freedom is also having the liberty to choose, the liberty to have a different perspective, and the liberty to confront if needed. If you don't have this kind of freedom, then you will find yourself in awkward situations that make it difficult for you to fulfill your commitments to your mentee. And that will hinder the health of your mentoring relationship.

## RELATIONAL ISSUES
The relational issues we've identified are: dependence, assumptions, money, cliques, and authority.

### Relational Issue #1: Dependence

As the relationship with your mentee grows, closeness will develop between you. You will become friends. And, as with all friendships, you will become more familiar with some mentees than with others.

However, as your relationship builds, dependency can begin to emerge.

This dilemma is not exclusive to mentoring relationships, but it is something to be taken seriously as a mentor. A mentor can become dependent on the mentee or the mentee can become dependent on the mentor. It works both ways. But as the mentor, it's your responsibility to be on the alert for anything that might lead either of you down that path.

When a mentee sees his or her mentor as the stabilizer in life, the mentee can grow dependent on that mentor and come to rely on him or her. In some respects, this is not a bad thing. But when it goes to the extreme, it becomes detrimental to the mentee's growth. As a mentor, you need to direct the person to God who is the true anchor and source of strength. Otherwise, you are contradicting the purpose of godly mentoring which is to enfold and engage one another in healthy relationships that empower and encourage personal growth and a vibrant relationship with God.

Whether the dependency becomes one-sided or mutual, it can begin innocently. It can also lead to either the mentor or mentee being overly demanding and possessive of each other's attention and time. This is unhealthy and will hinder the growth and benefit that can come from your mentoring relationship.

## Relational Issue #2: Assumptions

All of us make assumptions every day. Here are some that can create hindrances to a healthy mentoring relationship.

### Perspective is absolute truth

Wouldn't it be wonderful if we could believe everything everyone tells us; if we could believe that everything we hear is absolute truth?

In our mentoring relationships we want to believe what our mentees are saying to us, just as we want them to believe what we're saying to them. That's an honest relationship. That's friendship.

The reality is, however, that there are times when we have to assume that we aren't hearing all the facts. Our mentees may be telling the truth, but it's the truth through their eyes. In every situation, we must listen and not pass judgment. Yes, it's good for us to champion our mentees but we must also understand that they're speaking from one perspective—theirs. We're only hearing one side of the story, no matter how wonderful or horrible it may sound.

Be careful not to pass judgment on another person involved in the story (e.g., parent with child, business partners, husband and wife). Instead, support and encourage your mentee and spend time together to look at the situation from different perspectives.

### She's too busy to take time for me

Have you ever been told by someone that she thought you were too busy which is why she didn't invite you to something or didn't want to bother you with a problem she was struggling with? Sometimes people will see you as busy even if you aren't. You can't change that. But you can ask yourself, "What am I doing to give that impression? Do I always talk about all the things I have to do? What can I do differently to change that impression?" When people think you're too busy, it can keep them from asking for help when they really need it. And both of you miss out on a blessing.

A couple of weeks ago, I was taking care of details and packing to leave for a retreat where I was speaking for the weekend. I had lots to do and very little time to get it done. Right in the middle of hurrying around, someone on my women's leadership team at church called and wanted my perspective and advice on something that had happened to her the night before. When she asked if I had time to talk, I was honest, but I also made the point that she was important and I would be glad to take a few minutes to talk with her. Our conversation lasted about twenty minutes and by the end of the call she felt better and had decided on a course of action. I was happy to be there for her, and my deadlines were still met.

*Mentors always respond correctly*

Mentees can have the incorrect assumption that mentors always have the right answer or that they are always available. And when they don't live up to those expectations or beliefs, mentees can become crushed or disillusioned. In the mentee's eyes, the mentor's feet turn from iron to clay.

As mentors, we need to be sensitive to what has happened and choose a time to speak with our mentee about it. When we sense that we've offended our mentee, we need to exercise humility, acknowledge the offense, and apologize. We also need to use it as a learning tool to help deepen the mentoring relationship and forward the growth of our mentee.

When Donna was a teenager, she idolized her pastor's wife, who always had a listening ear. One day, Donna had something important she wanted to share, but when she approached the pastor's wife, she was in a hurry and couldn't take the time to even stop on the stairs for a minute to hear what Donna had to say.

When something like this happens, the temptation is to take offense, and one may even decide never to talk to that person again. However, when Donna talks about this event in her life, she reflects back on it as a time when she learned that it's not good to put people on a pedestal. Did she feel brushed off? Yes. Did she feel hurt? Yes, very hurt. But what she learned was that even the people we admire don't always live up to our expectations. They too have flaws.

**Relational Issue #3: Money**

In a movie called *The Money Pit* a couple purchases a home that they know requires renovation. When they start the work, they discover that there's more to do than they originally planned. With every wall that's removed and each floor board that's lifted, another defect is discovered and a new project is added to the growing list of needed renovations. The couple perseveres until they realize that their dream home has become a huge pit that swallows money.

There are a number of scenarios that could lead you or your mentee to feel as if you're throwing money into a pit. And though money can be a sensitive subject, it's important to address certain aspects of it here, in order to help avoid potential heartache or disaster.

*Business ventures*

If your mentee approaches you to go into a joint business venture with her, you'll do well to avoid it. Keep your relationship as a mentoring relationship and not a business partnership. It will save you a lot of potential grief and keep you focused on the purpose of mentoring.

*Co-signing*

My husband and I have, on occasion, been asked to co-sign for friends or family who were capable of handling loan payments, but needed a co-signer before they could be approved. In every case, we said no. I've heard heartbreaking stories of friends who co-signed for someone and a year or so later began receiving notices saying they were liable for payments that were not being met. We have never regretted saying no, even though it was sometimes difficult to do so.

*Financial need*

You may have mentees who ask you for assistance when they run into financial difficulties. But beware, it is not wise to loan money to your mentee.

This doesn't mean that you can't help someone financially if you know there is a desperate need. However, rather than a loan, you might consider giving the money as a gift. Even then, be wise and discerning.

> *Be wise as serpents and innocent as doves.*
>
> —Matt. 10:16b

When someone owes something to you, he or she becomes obligated or could feel an indebtedness that would change the dynamics of your relationship. Use the request as a teaching tool to deepen the mentoring, rather than turn the situation into a negative that could be detrimental to your relationship.

You may also consider using your mentee's request for a loan to help him develop a budget. If, however, this is not an area in which you feel comfortable, you could recommend options such as a book, a workshop, or someone else to help him learn to budget or manage his finances.

## Relational Issue #4: Cliques

It's natural for people who are involved in similar activities to want to be together. They share common interests, a common vocabulary, and common experiences. Teachers, medical personnel, truck drivers, and home schoolers speak the same language within their group. People in leadership gravitate to others who share in leadership. Musicians are drawn to each other. Sports competitors huddle together. And people who experience growth as a result of mentoring may want to share with each other.

The danger with cliques is that they exclude others and make them feel awkward. As your mentoring relationships grow in closeness, watch that they don't function to the exclusion of others. This can also lead to a form of dependency which we previously addressed as a hindrance to a healthy mentoring relationship.

**Relational Issue #5: Authority**

Assuming responsibility for your mentee's decisions and actions hinders the growth of your mentee and sets you up as an authoritarian figure. Neither is healthy. The mentee is dis-empowered and doesn't learn how to make decisions that are healthy. As the mentor, you too can become frustrated and even angry because your choices or decisions are not being fulfilled. The reality is that they are not being fulfilled because you ultimately don't have control over the outcome of the decision.

Scripture is full of references to individuals who challenged others or who made their own decisions, and took responsibility for them. They went down in history as men and women whom God used and blessed. Here are three for you to explore.

1.  Joshua 24:15-16—Joshua tells his people to, "Choose you this day whom you will serve." He left the responsibility to choose up to each individual.

2.  Ruth 1:15-16—Naomi tells Ruth to go back to her people, but Ruth refuses and chooses to follow Naomi instead.

3.  1 Kings 18:20-39—Elijah asks the Israelites, "How long will you waver between two opinions?" They said nothing so Elijah stood firm and alone in his belief.

The responsibility to make a decision is in the hands of each individual. If the mentee has not made the decision, he or she will not have a sense of ownership. Our goal is to teach our mentees to take responsibility and make decisions as we encourage them along the way.

Are you allowing your mentees to take responsibility for their decisions? Are you taking responsibility for your own decisions? It could be that you're pretty consistent in this area but maybe there's one choice you've been avoiding. Why not claim the words that Moses spoke as he passed the mantle of leadership to Joshua.

> *Be strong and courageous . . . It is the LORD who goes before you. He will be with you; He will not leave you or forsake you. Do not fear or be dismayed.*
>
> —Deut. 31:7-8

## Mentoring Moment

1. Are you more likely to anticipate or to adapt to circumstances or changes that occur in your life? How could you learn to do both?

2. In what area do you need to learn to be more flexible? What will you do to put this into practice?

3. Setting personal boundaries is difficult for many of us. When we realize that for everything we say "yes" to, we may need to say "no" to something else, we take an important step toward learning to set boundaries. What do you need to say "no" to in your life?

4. What relational issue do you need to work on in your own life? What steps will you take to improve in it?

# SECTION III

## The People in Mentoring

# CHAPTER 8

# The Heart of a Mentor

*Sometimes our light goes out but is blown into flame by another human being. Each of us owes deepest thanks to those who have rekindled this light.*

—Albert Schweitzer

THROUGHOUT OUR NEXT two chapters, we'll look at the attributes and disciplines of a mentor. But before we do that, let's see how the dictionary defines these two words:

- Attributes—Inherent qualities or characteristics ascribed to someone or something.
- Disciplines—Training expected to produce a specific character or pattern of behavior, especially training that produces moral or mental improvement.

In this chapter, we focus on the attributes or the fundamental qualities of a Christian mentor, which is the "being" that affects the "doing." And in the next chapter we will explore the disciplines or the ongoing development and "doing" of a mentor.

## God's Fingerprints

When I attended Bible school, I lived in a three-story dorm with sixty-five other young women. Our Dean of Women was a tall, gray-haired woman with a reputation for being a strict, no-nonsense individual. But, for me, Mrs. Folkvord always had a twinkle in her eye—even when she caught me pushing the rule book boundaries or instigating dorm pranks. I only wish I had taken more advantage of the years of wisdom she could have offered me.

I'll always remember the time I started a water fight in the dorm while everyone was supposed to be quietly studying in their rooms. It didn't take long for the fight to move from the third floor to the second as more girls entered into the fray. By the time Dean Folkvord walked in, the hallway was covered in water. Without a word, she surveyed the situation and seemed to know exactly who the culprits were. We braced ourselves for harsh reprimands which we'd be required to report on our weekly demerit sheet. Instead, Mrs. Folkvord calmly looked at us and said, "Well, girls, it looks like you have work to do. You know where the mop is." Knowing what I know today, I think she probably struggled to hold back laughter as she turned and walked away.

Mrs. Folkvord had the heart of a mentor and she left an indelible fingerprint on my life. Her example taught me that a calm response can often be more effective than a long lecture and stern look, although they too may have their place. She also demonstrated that what's in the heart of a person affects how she acts—even in the midst of foolishness. And that fun is fun, but one must be accountable and take responsibility for the outcome of the fun.

In Donna Otto's book, *Between Women of God,* she refers to the characteristics or attributes commonly seen in godly mentors as "evidence of God's fingerprints on their lives."[8] When I read that description, I envision a beautiful picture of God walking His fingers across our lives, as He tenderly holds us in His hand.

God held Mrs. Folkvord lovingly in His hand when her husband died and she came home from the mission field with her two daughters. His fingerprints were evident on her life as she walked through the loneliness of widowhood and committed her life to raising her children while guiding a dorm full of young women, day in and day out.

## All in a Day

Lifestyle mentoring means that it takes place every day, all day. It also depends on who is doing the mentoring as to whether or not it is based on godly principles. This understanding highlights how important it is that we focus on the heart of a mentor.

When I think back to the people who mentored me, I'm aware that their mentoring did not always have a spiritual focus. They taught me skills and demonstrated desirable qualities through which I benefited and I believe God used them in my life. But they did not all model a strong faith walk for me to follow. They mentored me from where they were in their own life journeys.

That said, let's be clear on two points. First, as Christians, God mandates that we all live godly examples. Therefore, in actuality, the attributes of a godly mentor are no different from what is expected of all Christians. Second, the quality of our relationship with God is vital.

As humans, we were all created in the image of God but that image was distorted because of sin. When we accepted Christ as our personal Savior, that distorted image was restored and we embarked on a lifetime of growing in Christ and becoming like Him.

*Therefore if any man be in Christ, he is a new creature: old things are passed away; behold all things are become new.*
—2 Cor. 5:17, KJV

If you have any doubt about where you stand with God, I urge you to talk with someone you know who has a personal relationship with Him, and who has lived that relationship in front of you.

When we accept God's Son, Jesus Christ, as our Savior, His Spirit is in us and we are in Him. We develop an intimate connection with Him, and the depth of that relationship determines how we live our lives.

As a Christian and as a godly mentor we are to be like Christ. We are not to be a false representation, but authentically Christ-like. This is the most important thing we could learn about the heart of a mentor.

## Being Christ-Like

Christ-likeness is rooted in our relationship with Christ through salvation and the indwelling of the Holy Spirit which produces spiritual fruit in the believer's life.

> *But the fruit of the Spirit is love, joy, peace, patience, kindness, goodness, faithfulness, gentleness, and self-control . . .*
> —Gal. 5:22-23, NASB

Put another way, Christ-likeness is the reproduction of the character and qualities of Christ in the life of the believer through the work of the Holy Spirit. To illustrate this definition, we need only to look at John 15 where Jesus talks about the vine and the branches.

> *I am the true vine, and my Father is the gardener. He cuts off every branch in me that bears no fruit, while every branch that does bear fruit He prunes so that it will be even more fruitful. You are already clean because of the word I have spoken to you. Remain in me, and I will remain in you. No branch can bear fruit by itself; it must remain in the vine. Neither can you bear fruit unless you remain*

*in me. I am the vine; you are the branches. If a man remains in me,*
*and I in him, he will bear much fruit; apart from me you can do*
*nothing. If anyone does not remain in me, he is like a branch that*
*is thrown away and withers; such branches are picked up, thrown*
*into the fire and burned. If you remain in me and my words remain*
*in you, ask whatever you wish, and it will be given you. This is to*
*my Father's glory, that you bear much fruit, showing yourselves to*
*be my disciples.*

—John 15:1-8, NIV

When Jesus says, "Come to me," He is inviting us to a relationship with Him. When He says, "Abide in me," He is inviting us to an ongoing and growing relationship with Him. Note that He is not saying, "Abide with me," which would be similar to saying, "Come walk alongside me." That could be a somewhat uncertain position. Rather, He is saying, "Abide in me." This is a solid, intimate relationship—Christ in us and us in Him. As we come to Him and abide in Him, the Holy Spirit reproduces the character of Christ in us, making us Christ-like.

In his book, *Abide in Christ*, Andrew Murray describes this relationship: "As earnest and faithful, as loving and tender, as the compassion that breathed in that blessed '*Come*,' was the grace that added this no less blessed, '*Abide*.'"⁹

It's almost poetic. Reverend Murray goes on to say, "It was not that He said 'Come to me and abide with me,' but, '*Abide in me.*' The intercourse was not only to be unbroken, but most intimate and complete. He opened His arms, to press you to His bosom; He opened His heart, to welcome you there; He opened up all His Divine fullness of life and love, and offered to take you up into its fellowship, to make you wholly one with Himself. There was a depth of meaning you cannot yet realize in His words: 'Abide IN ME.' And with no less earnestness than He had cried, 'Come to me,' did He plead, had you but noticed it, 'Abide IN ME.'"¹⁰

What a beautiful picture of intimacy. We are invited to a relationship with God, followed by the full desire of God to make that relationship complete, us in Him and He in us through the Holy Spirit reproducing the attributes of Christ in us. In short, becoming Christ-like.

As we become like Christ in all that we do and say, we walk the talk, we model a growing, authentic, transforming lifestyle of following Jesus.

This does not mean that we're flawless and never make mistakes. It does not mean that we live a life without struggles. It does, however, mean that we are consciously in the process of becoming more and more like Jesus. We are set apart—pursuing Christ-likeness and being transformed to "The Original" rather than being conformed to a counterfeit.

> *Do not copy the behavior and customs of this world, but let God transform you into a new person by changing the way you think. Then you will learn to know God's will for you, which is good and pleasing and perfect.*
>
> —Rom. 12:2, NLT

In Matthew 5:48 Jesus tells us to, "Be perfect, therefore, as your heavenly Father is perfect." The word "perfect" implies full development or growth into the maturity of godliness. It is not about being sinless. It's about authentically modeling Christ-likeness: being a living example of God's transforming power.

When we are authentically modeling Christ-like attitudes, we are not pretending to be Christ-like. We are becoming Christ-like. If we are only pretending, then we're simply putting on a show of Christ-likeness.

# Being Authentic

Some writers and philosophers explain authenticity as being honest with oneself, with God, and with others. Some understand it as getting to know who we are and being true to ourselves all the time without compromise. In other words, having our outside behavior, or lifestyle be consistent with who we are on the inside. However, if we define an authentic person as being someone who consistently lives or demonstrates through his or her behavior what he or she believes on the inside, then we would find many people to match that description. For example, Hugh Hefner of Playboy fame and Evangelist Billy Graham both appear to live a lifestyle that is consistent with what each believes, albeit on different ends of the lifestyle spectrum.

The *Merriam-Webster Dictionary* defines authenticity as "conforming to an original so as to reproduce essential features; an authentic reproduction; not false or imitation."

Sound familiar?

The Bible tells us that we are not to be a false representation. We are to be an authentic reproduction of Christ-likeness.

> *But just as He who called you is holy, so be holy in all you do; for it is written: "Be holy, because I am holy.*
>
> —1 Peter 1:15-16, NIV

It is possible for a person to say she is a Christian and still not live or model the authentic image of Christ. She says she believes one thing but her actions contradict her words. The reality of Christ in her life is covered up by how she, with ego and pride, chooses to live. The Holy Spirit is not given the freedom to reproduce the essential features of Christ in her.

Conversely, someone may present a Christian lifestyle but be far removed from it in his personal relationship with God. He is depending on his own efforts to be a Christian, rather than conforming to the image of Christ or modeling Christ-likeness.

The first person says she is a Christian but doesn't act like one. The second person knows he's not a Christian but tries to act like one. He may even be involved in the church and, dare I say, in leadership. Both are hypocritical. Both are not authentically reproducing Christ-likeness.

Where does that leave us? If anyone can claim authenticity, what difference does it make to us as Christians? What role does it play in who we are as mentors? Is it important to be authentic in order to effectively mentor and build valuable qualities into those around us? Or is authenticity just another well-used buzzword?

In his book, *Leadership*, Hudson Armerding, president of Wheaton College from 1965 to 1982, said that being an example is, "as if the trademark of God's name is on us and we therefore must be sure the trademark reflects the authenticity of the name we bear."[11]

As Christians, we have an awesome responsibility to reflect the authenticity of the name we bear. And when we truly pursue Christ-likeness, the Spirit of God is free to work in and through us.

When we mentor, we reach out with Christ-like authenticity. No agenda. No judgment. No ego. We practice the presence of God in what we do and say. We focus, not on mimicking what we think is Christ-like, but rather, on what Christ is reproducing in us. We become a living testament of God's redeeming grace. We model Christ-like authenticity from the inside out.

## Modeling Authentic Christ-Likeness

God is the Master Sculptor. When we surrender to His skillful hand, He chisels and molds us into the person He already knows is there—one who models Christ-likeness and who is able to effectively fulfill the purpose God intended.

It's much like a sculptor with a piece of clay. Everyone sees the clay as a blob of gray goop. But the sculptor knows what beautiful masterpiece can emerge.

In the late 1400s the people of Florence, Italy, looked at a large piece of marble and saw a weathered, pathetic hunk of stone from which a sculptor had tried to form a masterpiece some twenty years earlier. Unsuccessful, he discarded it. However, when Michelangelo, the upstart, rising star of Florence, saw the neglected stone, he saw the famous David statue. With loving and meticulous care, he chiseled away pieces of the marble that kept the David sculpture hidden within the stone.

When we invite the Master Sculptor to do His work in our lives, He begins to produce the character of Christ in us. As a godly mentor, our attributes reveal who we are in Christ. We are like pieces of clay in the Potter's hands—a work in progress as we become what the Master envisions.

If the attributes of honesty, trustworthiness, dependability, impartiality, authenticity, transparency, and openness are to be evident in our lives as mentors, then we must have a heart for God and surrender our will to Him.

We cannot be the mentor God wants us to be simply by taking courses, reading good books, or leaning on our own power. Our skills and experiences are useful, but if those are all we rely on, we will eventually slip up and/or run out of steam. To be truly effective over the long term, we must practice His presence, rest in His love, and abide in Him as He is in us. We must see others as He sees them. We must hear them as He hears them. We must focus our thoughts "on what is true, and honorable, and right, and pure, and lovely, and admirable." We must "think about things that are excellent and worthy of praise." (Phil. 4:8, NLT)

We can only be transparent and open with others when we allow ourselves to be vulnerable and surrender that vulnerability to God's strength and power. We can only be dependable when we surrender our independence to God. We can only teach from a place of spiritual wellness when we ourselves are teachable, surrendering our intellect and our judgments to the Master.

> *Anyone who listens to my teaching and follows it is wise, like a person who builds a house on solid rock. Though the rain comes in torrents and the floodwaters rise and the winds beat against that house, it won't collapse because it is built on bedrock.*
>
> —Matt. 7:24-25, NLT

> *Be honest in your evaluation of yourselves, measuring yourselves by the faith God has given us.*
>
> —Rom. 12:3b, NLT

## Mentoring Moment

Our relationship with God can easily become lost in the everyday busyness of life. In our desire to come alongside our friends and those we are mentoring, our own spiritual life can become routine and mundane, lacking joy, energy, and/or focus. To guide you through a spiritual health check up, prayerfully consider and journal your answers to the following questions.

1.  Think back over the last six months. Have you been living your life more by might and power, or by the Spirit? (Zech. 4:6)

2.  In what areas of your life do you need to be more Christ-like?

3.  What are you holding back that you need to surrender?

4.  Are you authentically modeling Christ-likeness or are you just pretending? What one step could you take to move you toward being more authentically Christ-like?

# CHAPTER 9

# The Disciplines of a Mentor

---

*We must not, in trying to think about how we can make
a big difference, ignore the small daily differences we can
make which, over time, add up to big differences that we
often cannot foresee.*

—Marion Wright Edelman

THREE OR FOUR years ago, I felt the need for a more meaningful prayer life and could have chosen any number of books to read on the subject. I even had some of the books in my own library. Instead, I contacted my friend, Eileen Enarson. Now well into her eighties, Eileen is a woman I respect and one who has mentored me informally for many years.

After I explained what I thought I needed, we agreed to meet for a period of three months. For exactly one hour every week, she guided me formally on the subject of prayer. Her insights led me to what I needed at the time. Today, I am grateful for her wise words and actions and still look to her as a godly mentor who practices the disciplines of a woman after God's own heart.

In the previous chapter, we identified the heart or inherent qualities commonly seen in godly mentors—attributes such as honesty, trustworthiness, dependability, impartiality, transparency, and openness. We determined that to be truly effective over the long term, we must authentically model Christ-like attitudes. And to do that, we must have a heart and will for God that is surrendered to Him.

In this chapter we will explore the personal disciplines of a mentor, which are defined as that which produces a specific character or pattern of behavior, especially moral or mental improvement. So, while attributes are the fundamental qualities or the "being" of an individual, disciplines are the ongoing development or "doing."

## Being Fit

Christian scholar and author Dallas Willard has written extensively on spiritual disciplines and says that, "we become like Christ by doing one thing—by following Him in the overall style of life He chose for Himself." He goes on to say, "We can, through faith and grace, become like Christ by practicing the types of activities He engaged in, by arranging our whole lives around the activities He Himself practiced in order to remain constantly at home in the fellowship of His Father."[12]

This does not mean that we only do what is Christ-like when people are watching, or when we're faced with a problem to solve, or when we need to respond to a specific situation. It means that we constantly practice the disciplines of being Christ-like, even when no one is around.

Think of a musician who performs beautifully on stage. Each note, rhythm, and phrase transports us into the experience and emotion that the composer felt as he was creating the music. The musician does not achieve this by simply picking up an instrument and making sounds with it.

A lot of behind-the-scenes rehearsing goes on prior to performing in front of an audience. And it continues on through each successive performance. No matter how many years a musician has performed, he must practice, practice, practice. By repeatedly going over the flow and tempo of the notes and rhythms, the life of the music is seared into the very being of the musician. It's this consistent discipline of practicing that enables him to deliver brilliant performances when he's on stage.

So it is when we practice disciplines that transform our lives into the likeness of Christ. As we exercise these disciplines behind the scenes and live a Christ-like lifestyle, we model a God-honoring, Christ-centered life for others to follow. Here are three disciplines to which I'd like to draw our attention: devour God's Word, devote yourself to prayer, and develop relationships.

## DEVOUR GOD'S WORD

I've found that in the most difficult times, the faster I get into the Word, the quicker I am lifted up out of the cruddy thinking that could so easily drag me down into a pit and keep me hostage there.

I've also discovered that when I feel my emotions going into a downward spin, a passage of Scripture often comes to mind. However, these verses don't come out of thin air. They come from spending time in God's Word—from reading, studying, and memorizing it.

*Faith comes from hearing, and hearing through the word of Christ.*
—Rom. 10:17

*But the one who looks into the perfect law, the law of liberty, and perseveres, being no hearer who forgets but a doer who acts, he will be blessed in his doing.*
—James 1:25

**God's Word at Work in Us**

Knowing God's Word in our minds is not enough. Yes, it increases our knowledge and we can recall it when we want to. But we also need to live it and to obey it. When we know and obey the Word of God, we can be more effective, godly mentors because the Word of God is working within us.

It makes us wise unto salvation.

> *From childhood you have been acquainted with the sacred writings, which are able to make you wise for salvation through faith in Christ Jesus.*
>
> —2 Tim. 3:15

It equips us.

> *All Scripture is breathed out by God and profitable for teaching, for reproof, for correction, and for training in righteousness, that the man of God may be competent, equipped for every good work.*
>
> —2 Tim. 3:16-17

It encourages us.

> *Blessed be the God and Father of our Lord Jesus Christ, the Father of mercies and God of all comfort, who comforts us in all our affliction, so that we may be able to comfort those who are in any affliction, with the comfort with which we ourselves are comforted by God.*
>
> —2 Cor. 1:3-4

It guides us.

> *Oh how I love your law! It is my meditation all the day. Your commandment makes me wiser than my enemies, for it is ever with me. I have more understanding than all my teachers, for your testimonies*

*are my meditation. I understand more than the aged, for I keep your precepts. I hold back my feet from every evil way, in order to keep your word. I do not turn aside from your rules, for you have taught me. How sweet are your words to my taste, sweeter than honey to my mouth! Through your precepts I get understanding; therefore I hate every false way.*

—Ps. 119:97-105

In short, when we immerse ourselves in Scripture, it renews our mind and keeps us focused. We can say, with the psalmist, "Thy Word have I hid in my heart that I might not sin against thee." (Ps. 119:11, kjv)

## How to Get Started

In his book, *The Life You've Always Wanted,* John Ortberg suggests how to get into Scripture and meditate on it. Here is a summary of that five-step process. It is a wonderful way to get started in devouring the Word of God so that it is active in our minds and hearts.

### Step 1: Ask God to meet you in Scripture

Before you begin to read, ask God to speak to you as you read and then expect Him to do it.

### Step 2: Read the Bible in a repentant spirit

When you read Scripture, read it with a vulnerable heart. Be prepared to be obedient and surrender everything to Him.

### Step 3: Meditate on a brief passage

Broad study of Scripture is valuable, but by immersing ourselves in a brief passage, specific words may stand out that we need to let sink into our heart. Ask God, "What do You have for me here?"

In the seventeenth century, Madame Guyon wrote, "If you read quickly, it will benefit you little. You will be like a bee that merely skims the surface of a flower. Instead, in this new way of reading with prayer, you must become as the bee who penetrates into the depths of the flower. You plunge deeply within to remove its deepest nectar."

*Step 4: Take one thought or verse with you through the day*

Choose a thought or verse from the brief passage you've read and recall it as you go about your daily activities. Think about it, pray it, and find ways to put it into practice.

*Step 5: Allow the thought to become part of your memory*

Memorizing bits of Scripture will help you when you need it. Don't think so much about how many words you are committing to memory. Think more about the difference they will make to your mind as you immerse it in Scripture.[13]

## DEVOTE YOURSELF TO PRAYER

David often cried to God when he felt his soul was being torn apart, when he felt hopelessly surrounded by enemies and didn't have anything left in himself to lead his people. The Psalms are full of the prayers of David agonizing before God. Yet, even though passages like Psalm 22 reveal his emptiness, they are also full of David's praises to God. He knew that God loved and cared for him, no matter what he said or did. And he knew that God accepted and loved him, just as he was.

Prayer isn't just about talking to God. It's also a way to be still before God. He already knows how we feel before we even open our mouths, so sometimes it's good to simply be still in His presence.

*The fruit of righteousness will be peace; the effect of righteousness will be quietness and confidence forever.*

—Isa. 32:17, NIV

There are times when I'm at a loss as to what to pray for or how to pray. There isn't anything inside me to even formulate a sentence. But God knows what's inside of me. It's okay for me to be quiet. It's that quiet time of simply being with Him and taking in His love that restores my soul. It lifts me up.

> *The LORD is my Shepherd; I shall not want. He makes me lie down in green pastures. He leads me beside still waters. He restores my soul. He leads me in paths of righteousness for His name's sake. Even though I walk through the valley of the shadow of death (or the valley of deep darkness), I will fear no evil, for You are with me; Your rod and Your staff, they comfort me.*
>
> —Ps. 23:1-4

## DEVELOP RELATIONSHIPS

God did not call us to be islands unto ourselves. He expects us to connect with each other and minister together. To that end, we see that relationships serve a number of purposes.

### Relationships Provide Wise Counsel

We are to seek wise counsel and not just wait for it to come to us. As we hear it, we increase in knowledge and we find safety. As we listen to wise counsel, we benefit from those who have walked before us. We are in the company of like-minded people. We are standing on the shoulders of giants.

> *A wise man will hear and increase in learning . . .*
>
> —Prov. 1:5, NASB

> *Where there is no guidance, the people fall; but in abundance of counselors there is victory.*
>
> —Prov. 11:14, NASB

*Timely advice is as lovely as golden apples in a silver basket.*
—Prov. 15:11, NLT

There are many ways God may choose to provide us with wise counsel. One way is through the books we read. I love books and usually have at least three or four going at the same time. God's Word is one of those books that is a valuable source of wise counsel. But if I do not take that wise counsel to heart, I am not listening. And Scripture is clear that fools "despise wisdom and discipline" (Prov. 1:7b, NLT).

Another way we can gain wise counsel is through the individuals God brings into our lives. I appreciate so much the people in my life to whom I can go for wisdom and advice. But one thing I've learned is that it's important not to just go to the people we think will tell us what we want to hear but also to the people who will tell us the hard things. We must also be sure that any counsel or words of advice that we receive, or that we give, are consistent with Scripture.

## Relationships Provide Accountability

As mentors, we can get so busy being available and walking alongside others that we forget the importance of being accountable to someone for our own spiritual well-being. Yes, we are, first and foremost, accountable to God. But He also placed us on this earth to walk together, to support, guide, and protect one another, and to be accountable to each other and those who are in authority over us. Accountability and connection to community are critical.

*But speaking the truth in love, we are to grow up in all aspects into Him, who is the head, even Christ, from whom the whole body, being fitted and held together by that which every joint supplies, according to the proper working of each individual part, causes the growth of the body for the building up of itself in love.*
—Eph. 4:15-16, NASB

### Relationships Provide Comfort and Encouragement

When we feel bruised or overcome with grief and despair, or are consumed by anger and frustration, it can feel as if we're fighting to stay alive or struggling to survive, as if we're on our own.

There have been times when I hurt so badly and felt so shattered and empty that I was sure I couldn't hold on any longer. On a couple of occasions I remember feeling so helpless that, as I cried with a friend, all I could say was, "Don't let me go. Don't let me go." It was as if I was hanging on to the end of a rope that was dangling over a deep dark pit and my only connection to getting out was that friend who was holding on to the other end of the rope.

Friends that we can trust during vulnerable times are priceless. They encourage us and support us faithfully. They challenge and love us unconditionally. And one of the greatest blessings is when we can, in return, be there for them when they need it.

> *Two are better than one, because they have a good reward for their toil. For if they fall, one will lift up his fellow. But woe to him who is alone when he falls and has not another to lift him up!*
> —Eccl. 4:9-10

## Staying Strong

A lot of what you do as a mentor requires that you give of yourself to others. If you are not constantly paying attention to your own spiritual health and relationship with Christ, you will burn out or find yourself wandering around in a wilderness—simply going through the motions or struggling to survive. It's important that you take time to renew and restore your heart, mind, and body so that you don't become tired and run down or give up.

What part of your spiritual health needs attention? What checkpoints do you have in place that connect you to community and keep you accountable?

*And let us not grow weary of doing good, for in due season we will reap, if we do not give up.*

—Gal. 6:9

As godly mentors, the practice of personal disciplines keeps us spiritually fit, enabling us to live in the fruit of the Spirit and model an authentic Christ-like life. When we devour God's Word, devote ourselves to prayer, and develop relationships with Christians who offer wise counsel, give encouragement, and keep us accountable, we are establishing disciplines that form a strong foundation from which to be an effective godly mentor.

## Mentoring Moment

1. Every day, for one week, follow John Ortberg's suggested five-step process as summarized in this chapter or as outlined in his book. Journal your experience.

2. How do you stay spiritually fit and strong? What, if anything, do you need to change in your life in order to be more spiritually fit?

3. Read Proverbs 2:1-10 and take note of the verbs used in the passage. How do these relate to the disciplines of a mentor?

# SECTION IV

## The Skills of Mentoring

# CHAPTER 10

# Using the Scriptures

*I thoroughly believe in a university education for both men and women; but I believe a knowledge of the Bible without a college course is more valuable than a college course without the Bible.*

—William Lyon Phelps

WHEN DONNA WAS growing up, she loved walking around Tubs Hill with her dad. One day she was sure she had struck it rich when she came across some rocks that had flickers of yellow in them. She rushed to her dad, proclaimed her great find, and was ready to stake her claim until he informed her that it was only fools' gold.

One of the ways we empower mentees is to teach them how to go to the gold mine of Scripture and find the pure nuggets that instruct and enrich their lives, rather than get taken in by theological fools' gold.

When Paul and Silas were sent to Berea, they began speaking in the synagogue and the Bereans, who had learned to do more than listen, searched the Scriptures to confirm what they were hearing.

> *Now these were more noble-minded than those in Thessalonica, for they received the word with great eagerness, examining the Scriptures daily, to see whether these things were so. Many of them therefore believed, along with a number of prominent Greek women and men.*
>
> —Acts 17:11-12, NASB

Adopting the Berean approach to learning protects us from the fools' gold of false teaching and religion that is all around us today. We need to ensure that what we believe and teach is not based on one verse that may be taken out of context but that it is consistent with the teachings of the whole Bible. We must learn to compare Scripture with Scripture.

> *Be diligent to present yourself approved to God as a workman who does not need to be ashamed, handling accurately the word of truth.*
>
> —2 Tim. 2:15, NASB

## Why Base Our Mentoring on Scripture

As Christians, many of us were spoon fed the Scriptures from the time we were children. Sadly, for most of us, that method of learning didn't change when we grew up. As adults, we listen to sermons, read books, and watch TV programs but may neglect to search the Scriptures for ourselves to find out if we're hearing its message correctly; or to hear what God wants to say to us.

The more we hear, without searching the Scriptures for ourselves, the more we become lazy and indiscriminately accept only what is being fed to us. We don't look at the context of the Scripture verses being used and we miss out on the complexity and richness of the Word. Our growth atrophies and we settle into stagnation.

Our goal in mentoring is not to have a person dependent on us to make his or her decisions, but rather to encourage total reliance on God, according to His Word. When we help a mentee find answers in Scripture, he is learning what God says and not just what our opinion is. The mentor maintains objectivity and the mentee learns to make choices based on Scripture. If there is a disagreement about what to do or not do, the argument is with God—not with the mentor. The result is that the mentee is empowered to grow on to maturity.

> *All Scripture is inspired by God and profitable for teaching, for reproof, for correction, for training in righteousness: that the man of God may be adequate, equipped for every good work.*
> —2 Tim. 3:16-17, NASB

> *For everyone who partakes only of milk is not accustomed to the word of righteousness, for he is a babe. But solid food is for the mature, who because of practice have their senses trained to discern good and evil. Therefore leaving the elementary teaching about Christ, let us press on to maturity.*
> —Heb. 5:13-14, 6:1a, NASB

As we read Scripture we see the words, "it is written," many times. This means that what you're reading in that passage relates to other writings in the Bible. The Old Testament kings and prophets, the New Testament characters, and Jesus all referred to Scripture in their teachings. Here are three brief samples:

## 1. Jesus
In John 8, we read the account of a woman caught in adultery and brought to Jesus for judgment. His response in verse seven was, "he

that is without sin among you, let him cast the first stone." This teaching of stoning the guilty is taken from Deuteronomy 17:7.

**2. New Testament**
In Acts 2, Peter quotes from the Old Testament book of Joel and the writings of David in the Psalms as a basis for his message at Pentecost. See Joel 2:28-32, Psalm 16:8-11, Psalm 110:1.

**3. Old Testament**
In 1 Kings 8:54-56, King Solomon quotes Moses when he stands before the people and blesses them. See Exodus 33:14 and Deuteronomy 12:10.

## Available Tools

Though Donna and I became Christians years apart and in different countries, God brought people into our lives who loved to study the Bible and who taught each of us how to apply it. Whether we met with them around a kitchen table or sat on the living room floor with Bibles open, men and women showed us how to search for the answers to our questions. They taught us not to take what they said as gospel truth, but to dig into the Scriptures for ourselves. It was there that we also began to learn how to use books like Bible dictionaries and handbooks, commentaries, and concordances.

> *Heaven and earth will pass away, but my words will not pass away.*
> —Mark 13:31

We get a chuckle out of the similarities we have discovered about our adventures in learning. For example, when Donna bought her first Bible at the age of sixteen, it was a *Scofield Reference Bible*. Fifteen years later, when I was nineteen, I bought my first Bible. It too was a *Scofield Reference Bible*. Since then, we have both added many study Bibles to our libraries, such as *The Ryrie Study Bible, Thompson Chain Reference Bible, Life Application Bible,* and *Parallel Study Bible.* These are just a few of the study Bibles that are available in many different versions.

The Internet also provides an endless library of sources such as www.biblegateway.com which enables you to look up any Bible reference in numerous translations. There are also computer programs like the *Zondervan Bible Study Library.* With all of these on-line resources, it is possible to eliminate some of the study Bibles and books from your bookshelves—unless, like me, you enjoy the best of both worlds.

In addition to the added helps of concordances, commentaries, and dictionaries, footnotes and cross references also serve as valuable resources, revealing a broader understanding and uncovering deeper truths found in a specific passage of Scripture.

As a mentor, you may be comfortable with the various study tools that are available, however, it's important to remember that not everyone is familiar with them. Therefore, don't assume that your mentee is. Be careful not to overwhelm him or her with too many verses or heavy study assignments.

Though there are many resources at our disposal, many people have never learned how to use them. If you are one of those people, you might want to find a class that covers the basics on how to study the Bible or find a willing mentor to guide you. Or you might suggest that your church, local Christian school, or bookstore host a seminar to introduce people to the study helps that are available.

## Resources to Assist in Personal Bible Study

In addition to knowing what Bible study tools are available, it's helpful to know for what purposes they are best used and how to use them. Here is a brief overview of basic study resources that I found in a brochure at my local Christian bookstore. Divided into three categories: location tools, context tools, and exposition tools, there is a short description of how each resource can be useful to your study. As you will see, some tools fall into more than one category.

## LOCATION TOOLS—HOW TO FIND IT

### Bible atlas (also a Context Tool)
Connects geography with how an empire expanded, whom they encountered and/or conquered, and what kind of culture they developed.

### Concordance
Considered the "gateway" book to biblical studies, this resource quickly and easily enables you to find any verse in the Bible. It also gives Hebrew and Greek origins but you will want to select one that matches your preferred translation.

## CONTEXT TOOLS—HOW TO UNDERSTAND IT

### Bible atlas (also a Location Tool)
Connects geography with how an empire expanded, whom they encountered and/or conquered, and what kind of culture they developed.

### Bible dictionary (also an Exposition Tool)
a) Recognized as an essential tool for basic study.
b) Alphabetically ordered to explain books, people, places, and significant terms found in the Bible.

### Bible handbook
a) Explains how the text, chapter, book, and whole Bible fit together.

b) Includes helps like: maps, fact-finder, and brief dictionary.

## Church history

a) Explores why the Bible is the way it is.
b) Helps to understand where denominations come from.
c) Looks at what lessons God taught through history.
d) Looks at how Jesus continued to change the world through His church.

## Cultural setting (also an Exposition Tool)

a) Explores manners and customs of the Bible.
b) Helps to understand and apply the cultural background of passages.
c) Helps to understand passages in the cultural context of the day rather than interpreting through our own cultural biases.

## EXPOSITION TOOLS—HOW TO EXPLAIN IT

## Bible dictionary (also a Context Tool)

a) Recognized as an essential tool for basic study.
b) Alphabetically ordered to explain books, people, places, and significant terms found in the Bible.

## Commentary

a) Explores the meaning of any text and significant issues within the text.
b) Helpful in systematic study of the Bible.

## Cultural setting (also a Context Tool)

a) Explores manners and customs of the Bible.
b) Helps to understand and apply the cultural background of passages.

c) Helps to understand passages in the cultural context of the day rather than interpreting through our own cultural biases.

**Word study dictionary**
a) Useful with your concordance.
b) Helps to explore the fuller meaning of individual words without having to know any of the biblical languages.

## Additional Tips on How to Use Scripture in Mentoring

1. Learn to know where to find appropriate passages and keep them in context.
2. Refer to a biblical character to recount a life lesson (e.g., This reminds me of . . . ) rather than try to recall a specific verse. If you know where the story is found you can tell your mentee so she can read it later by herself.
3. It's okay to communicate the principle behind a specific Scripture without quoting it word for word.
4. Don't bombard your mentee with Scripture verses. It will be easier for her to keep one appropriate passage in mind than to remember a whole list.
5. You don't have to answer your mentee right away. It's okay to say that you need to research something. It could also be a project that you do together.
6. You don't have to have all the answers.

## Mentoring Moment

If you are to teach someone else to dig into the Word for the answers to his or her questions and concerns, you must first be able to do it for yourself. What Scripture passages would you use to help guide your mentee if he or she said any of the following to you?

1. I have done so many things wrong that I don't think God could forgive me.

2. He hurt me so badly that I just cannot forgive him.

3. When I was eighteen I had an abortion and now every time I hear something about pro-life, I feel guilty.

4. When I think about how much time I waste, it makes me crazy. I really want to change but don't know how to go about it.

# CHAPTER 11

# Developing the Art of Listening

*The gates of our thought lives are primarily our eyes and ears.*

—Jerry Bridges

MY PATERNAL GRANDFATHER was a wonderful storyteller and poet. He especially loved to tell tales of his childhood in England and his adventures as a pioneer to Canada in the early 1900s. As a little girl, I loved to hear his stories. But when I became a teenager I stopped listening because, I reasoned, "I've heard Grandpa's tales so many times already. I can probably tell them myself."

Oh, the wisdom of a teenager.

Grandma, on the other hand, was the listener in their household. She had heard the stories many more times than my sister and me. But she had also learned how to deal with the repetition and how to read the signs of boredom on her young granddaughters' faces.

She would politely invite us to the other end of the room to look at something or take us for a walk to chat about "girl" things. But what I remember the most are the times she'd take us into her bedroom and open her special trunk filled with treasures. When she lifted the lid, the smells of age filled the room. Mothballed memories, musty keepsakes, and yellowed papers were carefully removed as she told us stories about lost loves and places we could only imagine.

There was one treasure she was especially attached to. With sadness on her face, she'd glance toward the bedroom door, tenderly lift a leather-bound book from the trunk, and explain, "This book was taken from me once and when I got it back, I promised I would never let it happen again while I was still alive." Then she'd lean toward me and my sister and quietly add, "If you love something, don't ever let someone take it away from you."

The book had been given to my grandma in 1916 by a woman named Mrs. Barrows, who asked her to take care of the book "until the last." I feel honored that, as my grandma neared the end of her life, she entrusted me with her leather-bound treasure of poetry called *The Value of Love* and asked that I take care of it just as she had done.

While Grandma visited with us over the old trunk, Grandpa probably thought we were still listening to him from the other room because, halfway through telling a familiar story to my dad, he would raise his voice and call to my grandma, "Isn't that right, Emma?"

She'd pause, smile at us with a twinkle in her eye, and simply reply, "That's right." Grandpa would then go on telling his story and Grandma would pull another treasure from the trunk.

Today, I wish I could sit and hear Grandpa tell his stories one more time. I know now that I would listen with greater interest. I would listen to his words as well as what he was saying between the lines. I'd hear sadness in his voice as he talked about his "lost little boy" who died of diphtheria when he was only ten. And I'd notice the mischievous boy in his eyes as he recounted his childhood adventures on the streets of nineteenth century London.

## Being a Master Listener

As mentors, one of the primary things we do is listen. Even being a good friend requires listening that is neither too passive nor too focused on solving a problem. Yes, some people are especially gifted listeners. However, no matter what kind of listener you are, you can develop your listening skills which will, in turn, help to maximize your mentoring.

In this chapter, we will look at the elements of listening, the levels of listening, and the hindrances to good listening. I encourage you to practice what you read here and watch the difference it makes in your everyday relationships.

## Elements of Listening

Our days are filled with conversation—talking, listening, texting, giving opinions, getting feedback. We chat. We email. We listen to words. We exchange ideas. We share our feelings. We interact.

The issue isn't whether or not we converse with each other. Rather, it's the quality or depth of the listening that we engage in. Where is our focus? Does the other person feel heard? What difference does our listening make in his or her life? When I took my coach training, I was taught that listening has two elements: awareness and impact.[14]

Here's how I apply this principle to mentoring.

### AWARENESS

This is the aspect of listening that gathers information through all our senses, including intuition, which is that God-given gift of being able to hear what God wants us to hear even when it's not obvious. And having the confidence to say what God wants us to say even if it sounds ridiculous to us at the time.

When we receive information, we hear, see, and experience what is going on around us. Our attention is focused on what we're receiving: words, smells, sights, sounds. Whether we're with someone in person or talking on the phone, we are able to notice differences in his voice, breathing, emotion, and energy.

As active listeners, we listen to what is being said; we listen for where the person is going with what he's saying; and we listen to what he's not saying—what's hiding beneath the surface. I like to call it listening between the lines. But there's more to listening than taking in information. We must also realize that the quality of our listening has impact, which is the second of our two elements of listening.

## IMPACT

This aspect addresses what we *do* with our listening. While our attention is still on the other person, we need to be mindful of the impact we have when we take action on our listening. The reality, however, is that while we take information in through all our senses, listening with anything but our ears can be a scary thing.

Think of it this way. If someone is telling you about something that is going on in her life, you are receiving information. The tone of her voice, the words she uses, and the expression on her face all contribute to the information you receive. However, the impact of what you do with that information is equally important.

Let's say that, as part of what you do with the information, your God-given intuition tells you to say something specific to your friend that sounds out of place. If you're like me, before you open your mouth, a few questions run through your mind. What if I'm wrong? What if I offend her? What if this thought is just a reaction to what I'm dealing with in my own life?

One evening I was attending a party where I didn't know anyone except the host, who introduced me to a young woman I'll call Mary. At first, our conversation was the typical surface stuff. But

I quickly sensed that Mary had more than the party on her mind. After we chatted for a couple of minutes, I asked a question that one wouldn't normally ask a person she had just met. I don't even remember what I asked. But I do remember that it had instant impact.

"Of all the things you could ask me, considering we just met, why did you ask that?" Mary said as she took a step backwards.

Before I could respond, someone interrupted us. But later, Mary took the initiative to come back to my question, and we ended up talking a lot about what was going on in her life.

I asked a specific question of a woman I had just met at a party where I didn't know anyone except the host. It was a risk. But when I acted on my God-given intuition the impact was major.

In short, awareness is what we receive—the words, the breathing, the pace (is it tentative or deliberate?), the tone (is it hard or soft?). On the other hand, impact is what we do with our listening. How we listen and what we do with the listening impacts the person we're talking with.

## Levels of Listening

In the past, you may have heard the levels of listening referred to as non-listening, passive, and active. However, the model I learned through The Coaches Training Institute, and which is described in the book *Co-Active Coaching,* refer to them as Level 1, Level 2, and Level 3. Each level builds on the other and together they broaden our scope of true listening.[15]

As you read about each of the levels, experiment with them and see what effect they have on you and on the person you're in conversation with.

## LEVEL 1

The focus of this level is internal. It's a learning level where we absorb information but our thoughts, opinions, and feelings are all centered on self. The impact is all on us. We don't notice anything or anyone else. If we're having an impact on someone else, we aren't aware of it because we don't notice anything but self. We hear what is being said but our focus is on our own ideas and opinions. In other words, it's all about me.

Imagine you're meeting with someone who wants to talk about a struggle in his life. As he pours out his heart to you, he is in Level 1, looking at himself. He's processing his thoughts and trying to understand his relationship as to what's going on around him. He's self-absorbed. And that's okay. It's an appropriate time for him to be in Level 1. But it's not the time for you as the mentor to be in Level 1.

If you're in Level 1 while you're listening, you will become sidetracked by what you're dealing with in your own life. You'll pay more attention to what you think—your opinions, your conclusions. You will be more concerned about where you want the discussion to go rather than focusing on where he is in that moment.

In the extreme, this makes it difficult to be fully present with what is being said or not said. It's as if you're not really there and the person's voice is just filling space.

## LEVEL 2

This level opens up our awareness and puts the spotlight on the person we're listening to. Our focus is directed "over there" on the other person. We listen actively to what he's saying and he feels seen and heard. We're also aware that we're having an impact on him.

Let's revisit the same example of you meeting with a friend.

Even though he is in Level 1, you are now listening in Level 2. Your awareness is totally on him—what he's saying, his body language, emotion, and expressions. You notice what he's not saying, what he is saying, and how's he's saying it. You see him in more detail. You see the twinkle or tear in his eye, the sorrow or smile in his voice. You are unattached to your own opinions and solutions and are, instead, focused only on the person who's talking to you.

When you respond to what you see and hear from him, your attention is still on him and you listen for the impact your response has on him. He is more reflective and speaks from his heart. He knows you're hearing him and he feels safe.

## LEVEL 3

While Level 1 listening is an internal focus and Level 2 is about having the spotlight "over there" on the other person, Level 3 opens everything up to a 360-degree view. Here the focus is on self, the person we're with, and the environment around us. We're aware of all three areas at the same time.

Level 3 listening is global. In other words, we're fully connected to the other person and we're together in the conversation. As the mentor, our awareness is everywhere and we take everything in: smells, sounds, emotion. When we listen at Level 3, we're relaxed and present in that moment.

To be effective at this level means that we must be very open. This involves being sensitive to our God-given intuition, which we address in the next chapter. Most actors, musicians, presenters, and comedians have an acute Level 3 listening sense. They can quickly assess a room and the temperature of the audience. They're able to determine what kind of impact they're having and then adjust accordingly. Their listening is very fluid.

For quick reference, here is a summary of each of the levels of listening.

## Illustration 3—Levels of Listening

| Levels of Listening—Quick reference guide | |
|---|---|
| Level 1— Internal Listening | • Attention is on ourselves—on the sound of our own inner voice<br>• We listen to our own thoughts, opinions, judgments, feelings, and conclusions<br>• Is an appropriate level for the mentee—not the mentor<br>• Can have negative impact on mentee if the mentor is listening from this level |
| Level 2— Focused Listening | • Attention is sharply focused on the other person—listening is directed at the mentee<br>• We're listening and watching for words, expression, emotion, what they don't say, their values, and what makes them come alive<br>• Is curious and asks powerful questions to go deeper<br>• Impact is on the mentee. Are they coming alive or becoming withdrawn? |
| Level 3— Global Listening | • We listen at 360 degrees<br>• Awareness includes everything: what we see, hear, smell, and feel<br>• Gives greater access to our intuition<br>• Impact is on the mentee |

## Bringing the Elements and Levels Together

To see how the two elements of listening and the three levels of listening come together, the analogy of a flashlight is very useful. Imagine . . .

1.  Awareness is the light
2.  Impact is where the light shines.

3. Level 1 is when you shine the light inward. Self is illuminated.

4. Level 2 is when you focus the light toward another person. You are curious. He or she becomes illumined and the impact is "over there."

5. Level 3 is when you allow the light to shine all around you. Everything in the environment is lit up.

## Hindrances to Good Listening

No matter how good we are at listening to others, at times we become distracted. We are intently listening but something diverts our attention away from the conversation. It's as if an internal button is pushed and our focus is broken.

### THE PAUSE BUTTON

Maybe you're one of those gifted—or plagued—people who can juggle many thoughts at the same time. You're at a party talking with a friend when you pick up on a conversation happening in a small group not far from you. You hear your name or catch a few words about something that interests you and your multi-task skills kick in. Your focus shifts from both ears and eyes paying attention to your friend, to one ear roaming off to the other conversation as your eyes wander to see who is talking. This all happens while you're trying to stay fully engaged in dialog with the person you're with.

Another version of the "pause" button is when we're distracted by our internal thoughts. Picture this. You and your mentee are comfortably seated in a coffee shop across from each other. You're listening to what she's saying until your memory interrupts and reminds you of something that's on your to-do list. It's at that moment that your internal "pause" button is activated and your attention is directed away from your mentee toward that something that screams to be heard.

## THE REPLAY BUTTON

How many times have you been listening to someone and, as she's talking, you're reminded of something similar that took place in your life? You try to stay focused and at least look like you're listening, but catch yourself mentally replaying your own experience. You would love to recount what happened to you but know it's probably not a good idea at the time. However, that doesn't stop your mind from going there. You become wrapped up in rehearsing your own story and miss out on what the other person is saying.

## THE PLAY BUTTON

Our lives are very full with no end of both mental and physical activity. As a result, life gets in the way of being able to take the time to be *with* each other or to *listen to* each other. We're too tired. We're out of energy. We're absorbed with what's going on in our personal lives and can't hear the pain or joy in someone else's words. Our "play" button is stuck because we don't stop. We neglect to give our minds, bodies, and spirits the rest they need so we can be fully alert to the spoken and unspoken needs of others.

## THE FAST-FORWARD BUTTON

This button is engaged more often than we like to admit. For example, you're in a conversation with someone and he begins to tell a story which you soon realize you've heard before. Or maybe you haven't heard the story but you have a pretty good idea where it's going. Your next move is to fast forward your mind to the end of the story.

How many of us have stopped listening because we presumed we knew what our friend (or our spouse or our child) was going to say. We tune the person out and begin planning what we'll say as soon as he stops to take a breath. When we do speak, we're totally oblivious to what he has just said.

*He who gives an answer before he hears, it is folly and shame to him.*

—Prov. 18:13, NASB

It's quite possible that you have, at one time or another, engaged one or more of these buttons. I know I have. When we are aware of the hindrances to good listening, understand the elements of good listening, and practice the levels of listening, we can be more effective listeners. Does this mean that we won't fall back on our internal buttons? No. The truth is that all of us are guilty of activating them from time to time. But we are also able to deactivate them when we choose.

## Mentoring Moment

1. Which of the four "hindrances to good listening" do you struggle with the most?

2. As you listen to your family, friends, mentees, or the people you work with, be mindful of what listening level you are using and journal what you learn from the experiences.

3. Read 1 Samuel 25. In this account of David's dealings with Nabal and Abigail, how do you see the levels of listening demonstrated?

4. Based on the same account, what do we learn about the results of developing the art of listening?

# CHAPTER 12

# Listening Between the Lines

*He who can no longer listen to his brother will soon be no longer listening to God.*

—Dietrich Bonheoffer

ONE MORNING, I was on the phone with a business owner who was overwhelmed with fear over a personal matter that threatened to change her life and deeply affect those close to her. This was not our first call and not the first time she had come to a coaching session in this frame of mind. I could hear the pain in her voice, as my mind ran through what I might say to help the situation.

Sounds a lot like level one listening, doesn't it?

My years of education and experience had given me tools and skills I could access, but we had done some of that on previous calls. Now what could I say? What could I do? I needed more than my own understanding.

As she talked, a passage of Scripture kept coming to my mind. For some reason, I had been drawn to the same verses every morning during the previous week. And now, there they were again, finding their way into our session. Was this God-given intuition or was I stuck in Level 1 listening mode? What if I risked referring to the passage and she got upset because I was quoting from the Bible? I didn't even know if she was a Christian, though she had said some things that made me think she might be.

My inner voice of doubt kicked in. "Don't say that. You could lose her as a client."

I quickly pushed the thought aside and refocused on her. But all through our call, the Scripture passage and a simple question kept intruding into my mind. As we neared the end of the call, it didn't feel as if we had accomplished anything, and the sound of her voice was still filled with fear and pain.

Finally I gave in and asked, "Have you ever read the book of James in the Bible?"

"Not for a long time," she replied.

Whew—got past the first hurdle, I thought. So far, so good.

Briefly, I explained that I couldn't get it out of my mind and in light of what she was dealing with, it seemed important that I bring it up. I then took another risk and challenged her to read the short book of James before our next call and consider the question, "What is surrender?"

The next week, she eagerly came to our call and said that she had done the reading in four different translations. And that began our exploration of what it is to surrender.

Imagine the world of possibility and discovery when we trust from a place where we don't have to know everything. A place where we have built on our relationship with God. A place where we can trust our God-given intuition to guide us. A place where we listen to others through God's ears.

# Applying God-Given Intuition

The pursuit of knowledge and new skills provides us with valuable resources and opens up new experiences to explore. Some of us might even say that we're driven to learn. We stretch and grow, we broaden our horizons, and we apply the tools and principles that we gain along the way.

Personally, I put a lot of value on growth. I love to learn new things and help others grow. And my assumption is that you are similar because you're reading this book.

The Bible is full of references to knowledge and wisdom.

*Joyful is the person who finds wisdom, the one who gains understanding.*

—Prov. 3:13, NLT

*Wise people treasure knowledge, but the babbling of a fool invites disaster.*

—Prov. 10:14, NLT

*A mocker seeks wisdom and never finds it, but knowledge comes easily to those with understanding.*

—Prov. 14:6, NLT

For all the good things we read about knowledge, the Bible also warns us about the pitfalls of knowledge and cautions us about the abuse of it.

*Don't be impressed with your own wisdom. Instead, fear the LORD and turn away from evil.*

—Prov. 3:7, NLT

*But while knowledge makes us feel important, it is love that strengthens the church. Anyone who claims to know all the answers doesn't really know very much. But the person who loves God is the one whom God recognizes.*

—1 Cor. 8:1b-3, NLT

Over the years, as I've coached, mentored, and led teams and individuals, I've discovered that it's easy to fall back on what I've learned along the way and to draw on tools, principles, or simple steps in order to solve a problem. But that's not what God intended.

In the first letter to the Corinthians, the apostle Paul says that what he had to say was not based on his own wisdom, but it came through the power of the Holy Spirit. This was significant so that the faith of the Corinthians would not rest on the wisdom of man but on God's power. So it is for us. God intends that we not rest on our own wisdom, but on His power.

*My message and my preaching were not with wise and persuasive words, but with a demonstration of the Spirit's power, so that your faith might not rest on men's wisdom, but on God's power.*

—1 Cor. 2:4-5, NIV

Listening to our God-given intuition is not about working hard or analyzing the information that we receive as we talk with a mentee. It's about rest and trust. It's about believing that God is in control. It's about being confident that God will direct our thoughts, actions, and words to bring about the impact He wants.

Yes, education and experience are valuable, but we are not to depend on them alone. God created us with a mind to learn so I believe He expects us to use it. At the same time He also instructs us not to lean on our own understanding.

*Trust in the LORD with all your heart and lean not unto your own understanding; in all your ways acknowledge Him, and He shall direct your paths.*

—Prov. 3:5-6, KJV

# The Role of Curiosity

As we acknowledge that all wisdom comes from God, He directs our thoughts and words so we can more effectively serve Him. He will show us how to form stronger relationships and mentor at a deeper level. But our relationship with Him is key in this process.

I also believe that God created us with a sense of curiosity that He can use. Curiosity allows us to dig below the surface of what our mentee is saying, to where her thinking is coming from, and to what her perspective is on an issue. When we listen and are curious, we don't need to have all the answers.

*We can gather our thoughts, but the LORD gives the right answer.*

—Prov. 16:1, NLT

Imagine what might be open to us if we didn't pretend to have all the answers or think we had to have all the answers. Imagine the opportunities that might surface if we didn't let life, or our to-do list, get in the way of taking time to be curious or of listening at Level 2 to someone who needs to talk.

Three things hinder us from listening at Levels 2 and 3, which is where curiosity plays an important role. One is our ego. We want to be sure people are aware that we know our stuff and that we know what we're doing or we understand what they're talking about. This type of thinking closes the door to conversations that have impact. And it keeps us listening at Level 1 as described in the previous chapter.

The second hindrance that keeps us from being curious is when we're in too much of a hurry. We're concerned that, if we ask a friend a question that digs deeper into something she's said, she might take too long to answer it. And then we'll feel obligated to listen, even though we'd rather move on to something or someone else. We don't want to take the time.

The third hindrance to effective curiosity is when we're afraid that the answer to our question might take us into uncomfortable territory. We think she'll become too emotional or we'll be reminded of some pain or sadness in our own lives. And we're not prepared to go there.

As mentors, we may be asked for feedback, advice, or an opinion. But many times a listening ear is all that is needed. Curiosity is part of being an active listener.

> *Oh, that I had someone to hear me!*
>
> —Job 31:35a, NIV

> *Be happy with those who are happy, and weep with those who weep.*
>
> —Rom. 12:15, NLT

## Listening Makes a Difference

Over and over again, people tell me they want to make a difference, to leave a mark or a legacy. But the question is whether or not they are ready to do what it takes to make it happen.

Making a difference involves building relationships; and building relationships requires time with people where, more often than not, it matters less about what we say or do and more about how we listen. As society has grown more independent and our lives have become busier, it is the deliberate act of listening that has deteriorated.

Listening is not about having half an ear on someone who's talking to us while we check mail or text messages because we think we know what he's going to say. It's not about formulating how we'll respond once he finishes talking. And it's not about being lost in our own thoughts.

Listening is a door into another person's life. It's something to be treated with respect. When we truly listen, we see people through God's eyes. We hear them through God's ears. We give them permission to be themselves. And we accept them for where they are at any given moment.

In the same way that you want people to feel relaxed when they walk through the door of your home, a mentor who really listens provides a special place for another person to relax and to be himself or herself.

When we listen through God's ears, people feel welcomed and loved. That means that when we listen, we must be brave enough to be honest. It means we focus on them, not us. It means we are curious, not defending or justifying. It means we let go of our own fears and limitations so we can come from a place of creativity, possibility, and excellence. It means that we always ask what will move people forward and help them grow into the people God intended them to be.

## Listening Is Biblical

We miss so much when we don't listen—really listen. Yet Scripture is very clear that God expects us to focus on Him and to listen to each other.

### FOCUS ON GOD

We are to focus on God, who is the Great Listener. We are to read His Word and be still. Take time to listen and give Him a chance to speak.

*Incline your ear and come to Me. Listen, that you may live . . .*
—Isa. 55:3, NASB

Are you taking time to listen to God? I mean to really listen. Or is your time with Him a quick listing of request after request which ends with, "Okay, God. That's about it for now. Please go with me through this day."

God calls us to listen. Listen to His wisdom. Listen to His correction. Listen to His direction. And listen to each other.

## LISTEN TO EACH OTHER

There are many passages of Scripture that talk about listening to each other. In fact, God sees it as important enough to lay it out as a direct admonition.

> . . . let everyone be quick to hear, slow to speak and slow to anger.
> —James 1:19, NASB

Theologian and pastor Dietrich Bonheoffer, who was executed in a Nazi concentration camp for his outspoken beliefs, said it beautifully in his book, *Life Together.*

> Just as love to God begins with listening to His Word, so the beginning of love for the brethren is learning to listen to them. . . . Many people are looking for an ear that will listen. They do not find it among Christians, because these Christians are talking when they should be listening. But he who can no longer listen to his brother will soon be no longer listening to God either; he will be doing nothing but prattle in the presence of God...
> —Dietrich Bonheoffer (1909-1945)[16]

I love that word "prattle." How many times do we "prattle" in the presence of God? We are so self-absorbed that we can no longer listen to others. And before we know it, we're no longer listening to God either. All we can do is prattle.

Think about how different our society would be if we truly listened to one another. How about our churches? What difference would it make if we listened to each other? Or what about our families and friends? What would happen if we took the time to listen?

## Mentoring Moment

1. What can you learn about listening from these passages? Job 34:3, Proverbs 15:23, Proverbs 16:1, Isaiah 50:4

2. What personal qualities do the following Scripture passages say are important? Which of these qualities do you believe God wants you to grow in, especially in the way you listen to others? James 3:17, Colossians 3:12, Galatians 5:22-23

3. From the following verses, what can you learn about how God listens to us? Exodus 3:7, Deuteronomy 26:7, 2 Samuel 22:7, Psalm 34:6, Psalm 34:15-18, Isaiah 65:24, Psalm 6:8-9, Psalm 10:17, Psalm 34:17, Psalm 145:19

# CHAPTER 13

# Applying the Power
# of Questions

*The most powerful tool mentors bring to the mentoring
relationship is the provocative question.*

—Walter C. Wright

A S MENTORS, IT'S important to know that being a good
listener requires more than our ears. It requires our ears,
our eyes, and our hearts. It requires all of us. It also requires
that we know when to listen and when to speak, moving seam-
lessly from one to the other like dancers and musicians who flow
freely from one movement to another and from one progression
of notes to the next.

Dancers listen to the music. They know when to start and when
to stop. They know what moves to use and when to use them.
They are present with the music and the spirit of the music. They
dance in the moment.

Musicians know how to listen, when to play, and what to play.
To an outside observer, the sounds effortlessly blend together to
form beautiful music. Or at least we hope they do. When musicians
have a jam session they play what they hear and feel, and all without

sheet music. The music is fluid. The musicians are spontaneous. They play in the moment.

But dancing or playing in the moment doesn't just happen. Musicians, who are able to ad-lib or sit in on a jam session, do it from experience and knowledge. They've learned the basic rudiments and scales. They've listened and learned. True, for some a lot of it comes naturally. But even a naturally-gifted musician benefits from learning the basics. And that's exactly how it works with mentoring. It's impossible to perfect something if we don't practice. So we learn, we practice, we do. And we learn and practice some more so we can do it even better.

When my son, James, was fourteen, he asked me to teach him how to play the drums. Having played since I was twelve, I had continued drumming during my pregnancies which meant that he had heard the music of the drums since before he was born.

As a young teenager, James had his eyes on the big, black, shiny drum set sitting in our family room. I think he assumed Mom would show him some cool moves and then he'd be able to jam with his friends. What he didn't expect me to do was to hand him a well-worn sheet of paper that I had used almost thirty years earlier.

"Okay, let's start with the first line," I said.

When he realized I was serious, I explained that once he learned the first basic rudiment of drumming, we would continue on down the page until he could play all of them.

I knew that if he learned the rudiments, he would soon be able to automatically flow from basic rhythms to more complex riffs. He'd have the freedom to learn any style and play anything he wanted on the drums. And he does.

That's the way it is for us as mentors. We take what we learn and apply it as we go. If we learn the basic skills well, we're able to figuratively dance in the moment with our mentees. Over the next three chapters, we'll apply the art of well-timed words as a means of helping create fluid conversations, deepen our mentees' learning, and empower them in their growth.

## Asking Powerful Questions

Prior to becoming a professional coach, I didn't ask a lot of questions. Instead, I thought about the question and then hunted for the answer on my own. In retrospect, I think there were three reasons for that.

One, I really didn't want to take the time to listen to the detailed answers I expected to get in return. How's that for a good example of Level 1 listening? Two, I often thought my questions were too simple and that they might be seen as unintelligent. Three, I thought I was supposed to already know the answer, so if I asked the question, people would think I didn't know anything.

In my life journey, I've discovered that one of my core values is adventure and that asking powerful questions honors that value because questions reveal intriguing places to explore. Questions stimulate all kinds of thoughts that may not have come up if I hadn't stepped into the unknown and asked a question. I've also learned that questions are an integral part of listening, building mentoring relationships and empowering mentees.

I remember a coaching client who would regularly respond to my questions with, "I don't know." It didn't seem to matter whether I started the question with how, what, or why. He would always answer, "I don't know," and then wait for me to tell him what to do.

Eventually I learned to present the question in a different way. When I asked him, "What do you see yourself doing in three years?" and he responded with, "I don't know," I said, "So—what does your future self say about it?" On one occasion, after he had responded in his usual way I asked a simple, five-word question, "What are you afraid of?" That question opened up new opportunities to talk about how he can be more decisive and responsible for his attitudes.

More than anything else, a good mentor needs to be skilled in guiding the conversation with a mentee. And an excellent way to do that is to know the difference between a poor question and a powerful question and when to speak and when to be quiet. Here are some guidelines to follow.

## BE PATIENT AND PERSEVERE

It's easy to fall into the trap of thinking that we need to fill the silence that follows a question, especially if the mentee says, "I don't know." Asking a powerful question can necessitate perseverance and patience, especially when we know the answer or think we know what he or she should do. It's tempting to break silence and tell him or her what to do. It also feeds the ego to think that someone wants to hear what we think are words of wisdom. But beware. This is not empowering your mentee or helping him take responsibility for his decisions and actions. It is not helping him grow.

> *Let no man deceive himself. If any man among you thinks that he is wise in this age, he must become foolish, so that he may become wise.*
>
> 1 Cor. 3:18, NASB

When you've asked a powerful question, don't be afraid of the silence that may follow. It's a lot more powerful if you pause, give your mentee time to adjust to the impact of the question, and wait for a response.

## BE CURIOUS AND COURAGEOUS

Asking powerful questions also requires us to be curious and courageous for the benefit of the person we're mentoring. When we're curious, we learn more about each other. We build trust and confidence in each other. We draw our mentee out and guide him in using the wisdom God has given him. Being curious, however, is not about asking for more information. It goes deeper than that, deeper than asking for details that we really don't need to know.

Courage, on the other hand, may mean we need to interrupt the other person so as to get to the heart of the matter. Or it may involve being brave enough to ask a question that we think might be risky or might make us sound ridiculous.

## USE SHORT AND PROVOCATIVE QUESTIONS

The more direct a powerful question is, the more effective it will be in deepening our mentee's learning and giving our conversations purpose. Asking a short, two-word question such as, "So what?" may sound elementary and almost combative but, when asked in the right way, it can stop someone in his tracks so that he no longer evades, justifies, or rationalizes, which is what he may have been doing for years.

Although Scripture doesn't reveal that Jesus asked a lot of questions, the ones it does reveal show that they were to the point and they were effective. They stimulated more questions and discussion. They invited listeners to look deeper, not just with their intellects but with their hearts.

When Jesus asked His disciples in Matthew 16, "Who do you say that I am?" His question took Peter beyond his intellect and past other people's speculations so that he answered with his heart, "You are the Christ, the Son of the living God." Jesus' response to his answer was, "Blessed are you, Simon Bar-Jonah! Flesh and blood did not reveal this to you, but My Father who is in heaven." I wonder what would have happened if Peter had not listened to what God was telling him in his heart.

## USE OPEN-ENDED QUESTIONS

A closed-ended question is one that may need only a "yes" or "no" or a one-word answer. It doesn't lead anywhere. On the other hand, an open-ended question invites introspection, stimulates creativity that may uncover other possibilities, and often leads to another question.

Think of an open-ended, powerful question as part of an intricate road system that leads to other roads, adventures, and discoveries. The possibilities are endless. Each crossroad or each fork in the road poses a question that, depending on the answer, can lead you and your mentee on a wonderful journey of discovery and take you deeper into a meaningful conversation that will encourage your mentee's growth.

Here are two examples to illustrate the difference.

**Example #1**
Closed-ended: Do you plan to launch this new ministry without people or funds available to help you?
Open-ended: What would it take to make this new venture happen?

**Example #2**
Closed-ended: If your life depended on exercising every day, would you do it?
Open-ended: What would you do if your life depended on making a physical lifestyle change?

In Luke 18:41, Jesus used an open-ended question. To the blind man he asked, "What do you want me to do for you?" He didn't ask, "Do you want me to tell these people to stop pushing you aside?" or "Do you want to come with me?" He simply asked, "What do you want me to do for you?"

Asking closed-ended questions can lead to a frustrating dead-end. However, asking an open-ended question like, "What do you want?" invites the other person to explore. It presents a myriad of possibilities and enables your mentee to look at an issue through different lenses and respond from his heart.

The blind man could have rationalized his desire to be healed by telling himself what others may have been telling him all his life—that he would always be blind. Or he could have said, "I don't know." But instead, he responded from what he knew deep in his heart. More than anything else, he wanted to see and he believed that Jesus could make that happen. He replied, "Lord, I want to see!"

## Ten Tips on Asking Powerful Questions

When using questions to guide your mentee, here are some helpful tips.

1. Don't presume where your mentee is going in the conversation. Dance with him or her wherever he or she leads you.
2. Listen carefully to what your mentee says and use one or two of his or her words to form your question.
3. Ask one question at a time and keep your questions simple.
4. Refrain from asking "why" questions which can sound judgmental and tend to put people on the defensive.
5. When mentees ramble on, it may be because they're afraid to go to the heart of the matter. A well-timed question can guide them to the core of the issue.
6. As the mentor, we don't have to understand everything about the situation.
7. Let go of the need to be right or of having to get what you perceive to be the right answer.

8. A good question will always send your mentee some place in his or her thinking and emotions. Where do your questions send your mentee?

9. A good question will likely be followed by some silence. Don't be afraid of it.

10. Not everything has to be a question.

## One More Thought

Imagine an airplane pilot sipping coffee as she relies on the autopilot to fly the plane. Everything is going smoothly until a gauge on the instrument panel flashes and an alarm sounds. The pilot realizes she must take the plane off automatic pilot.

A well-placed, powerful question is like that. It's a sudden flash that forces people off autopilot and jars them away from familiar thinking or actions they've grown comfortable with.

When we rely on God's power rather than our own understanding, we can be sure that He knows everything about the situation our mentee is in and the best way to address it. His power is far greater than our intellect or understanding. We can rely on Him for everything, including how to word the question.

Imagine the difference that a well-placed, powerful question could make in the life of a man who is thinking of giving up on his marriage, or a teenager who is struggling about what to do with her life, or a woman who is grieving the decline in her health. What new possibilities or perspectives could open up with just the right life-changing question—a question that is inspired by the unchangeable God who changes lives?

## Mentoring Moment

Write a closed-ended and an open-ended question for each of the following scenarios.

1. Your mentee has just told you that her son ran away from home last night.

2. A young woman excitedly told you that she has a job opportunity as a live-in housekeeper to a thirty-year old bachelor.

3. Your mentee said, "I'm going to quit university and go on a three-month expedition across China."

4. A young man has just told you that he plans to go live as a homeless person for a month.

5. Your daughter asks to move home because her husband walked out on her.

# CHAPTER 14

# Recognizing the Time for Action

*If you want to reach the sky, you have to learn how to kneel.*
*Do not hold on to the trivia that binds you to mediocrity.*

—Steve Nicholson

JACK WAS A gifted young man whose passion for life and for people, along with his desire to achieve great things, drove him to succeed at whatever he did. His all-or-nothing approach to life also carried over to the business coaching he asked me to do with him.

One of the first things we worked on was to help him identify and articulate his personal core values. However, during the process, Jack dismissed a value that he had initially been passionate about. My God-given intuition and experience told me that this confident, take-action man was avoiding something and letting fear get the best of him.

To help him break through this wall, I first asked some specific questions to confirm my suspicions and to see if we could get to the root of the issue. Listening carefully to Jack, I then drew on one of the three tools we will cover in this chapter: query, request, and challenge. Having first learned these skills and those in the following chapter through The Coaches Training Institute, I have since adapted them to mentoring and used them widely.

As we neared the end of one of our sessions, I could have given Jack a *query* to take home and think about, or made a *request* of him to help him discover something new, or given him a *challenge* to stretch him beyond his comfort zone. Each of these options is a useful skill to help a mentee learn and grow. However, every person is different, which is why it's important for us as mentors to keep an open mind and be sensitive to what will best serve our mentees. One size does not fit all.

Because of the kind of person Jack was, I knew that he would respond well to doing something on the spot and wouldn't object to closing his eyes.

"Jack, close your eyes and imagine you're walking down the busiest street in your city. We'll call you "Today Jack." Now imagine that one of the people walking toward you is your future self ten years from now. We'll call him "Future Jack." As your steps bring you closer to Future Jack, what do you think he would tell Today Jack not to miss during the next ten years of his life?"

Tears ran down Jack's cheeks and he opened his eyes. He got the message.

That day changed everything about how Jack did his work and how he approached his life as a husband and father. Later, his wife told him that she'd been waiting for years for him to recognize and accept that value that she knew was part of him.

Remember that each mentee is unique and that, while one will benefit from a certain type of approach or skill, another mentee may benefit from something altogether different. The skill, or tool, that I used with Jack, is referred to as a request. However, someone else in a similar situation may have been better served by a query or challenge.

Let's take a look at these three action tools in more detail.

## Leaving a Query

When you end a mentoring session, you can guide your mentee's learning between the sessions by leaving him with a query that gives him something to think about as he integrates the learning into everyday life.

Giving your mentee a query is much like asking a powerful question. However, it cannot be answered all at once, which is why it's generally given as homework. A query needs to simmer in his mind and is meant to be thought-provoking. It allows the mentee to be curious, to examine it from different perspectives and to come up with different possibilities.

When you come to the next mentoring session, talk about what your mentee discovered as he pondered the query. Use his response to go deeper, exploring what he is learning from it.

Here are some sample queries:

1. What is it to be a leader?
2. What are you tolerating?
3. What is it to be afraid?
4. What is it to surrender?
5. What is control?

The query is a great way to get below the surface of what is really going on with your mentee. It makes him think. It challenges him to reflect on areas that may be difficult. It's a wonderful tool to help him get past what may be holding him back from being the person God created him to be. Here's an example.

Ruth was a business woman who was under a lot of stress but had trouble letting go of what stressed her. At the end of one of our sessions I left her with the query, "What is control?"

The next week, Ruth told me what she had discovered and said that she had created something to illustrate the results of her discovery. Remember, I did not tell her to create something; I simply asked her to think about what control is. It was her decision to take the question further.

It's important to let our mentees work through what the question means to them, without a step-by-step, how-to list from us. If we give them more than the query, it could limit their thinking and creativity.

Ruth's visual representation of control was a tightly woven mess of rubber bands the size of a tennis ball. To her, this jumbled ball showed how she felt about having to stay in control of everything but that in reality she didn't feel like she had control of anything. This realization began a journey we took together as she learned how to prioritize and let go of what she could either delegate or dismiss as unimportant. She also gained an understanding of the difference between healthy and unhealthy control.

## Making a Request

A request is not about what the mentor thinks the mentee should do. Rather, it is a suggestion made by the mentor in the service of the mentee. It's meant to move the mentee toward taking action and learning at a deeper level.

You will find that some mentees respond to a request with excitement at the opportunity to do something they believe will help them grow. Others hesitate with, "I don't know if I can do that." Either way, a request is meant to have an impact on the mentee.

I've found that if a mentee accepts all the requests I give him, it usually means I need to up the ante and give him stronger requests. Regardless of the level of request, the goal is to help your mentee discover new learning that he can apply to his growth. Here are two examples and the impact the requests had on a couple of my mentees.

## EXAMPLE #1

**Background:** For Sam, freedom was a personal value he took seriously and did not want to compromise. He was struggling with keeping priorities organized in his life and fulfilling his responsibilities to his family and business. However, enjoying a sense of freedom was important to him. After talking about the tyranny of the urgent and explaining that he felt as if everything in his life was bound by a heavy chain with multiple links, we talked about perspectives and options. At the end of the session, I made a request that may sound strange to you, but it worked for him.

**Request:** Find a picture of a big ax and write "freedom tool" across it. Put the picture near your desk where you will always see it and use it as a visual reminder of whether or not the task you're facing is important or if it can be "axed."

**Impact:** Sam didn't wait until our next session to let me know what happened. He was so excited that he contacted me later that day to say that he had fulfilled the request and that instead of putting a paper picture on his desk, he had created a screen saver of an ax for his computer. He was already using it to help control his chain of "must-do links" that had threatened to choke him and take away his freedom. Connecting his list of "must-dos" to his value of freedom helped him put things in perspective and bring a renewed sense of balance to his life.

## EXAMPLE #2

**Background:** Steve had great aspirations for his future, but was having trouble with what he was and wasn't doing to achieve them. He struggled with the kind of person he felt he had to be in order to get to where he wanted to go with his life. He was stuck.

**Request**: Write yourself a letter from your future self, telling your present self how you got to where you are ten years from now.

**Impact**: Steve experienced phenomenal breakthroughs with this request. When he wrote that letter as if it was from his future self, he was able to step back to see what was holding him hostage and what he had to do differently to get to where he saw himself going. One phrase in his letter, which he gave me permission to use, said, "If you want to reach the sky you have to learn how to kneel. Do not hold on to the trivia that binds you to mediocrity."

Sometimes our mentees are trapped in attitudes and thinking that they've learned to live with. They don't like it, but they tolerate it. That's bondage. And that's exactly where Satan wants to keep us. He knows that if he can keep us discouraged or afraid or disillusioned, he has won. But God hasn't given us the spirit of fear. The spirit of fear comes from Satan. God has given us the spirit of power and of love and of a sound mind (See 2 Tim. 1:7).

As we make requests of our mentees, we help them break past the limitations and lies so they can see and experience the power of God at work in their lives.

## Delivering a Challenge

Most of us have, at one time or another, been stuck in one perspective, or in the current reality of what is possible. It's like the forest and the trees scenario. Nothing is clear. We can't move beyond where we are because all we see is what we know. We only see what's in front of us at the time.

The purpose of giving our mentee a challenge is to break up that reality and perception of what is possible. And a well-timed challenge does just that. It stirs things up.

When you deliver a challenge that takes your mentee's breath away, don't be afraid of it. Trust your intuition. It may be just what she needs to move her out of her comfort zone and help her grow. Here's an example.

As our session neared the end, I began to give Sheila an inquiry. But instead of an inquiry, God planted a challenge in my mind and sent it out of my mouth before my brain could say no. I heard the words I was saying but they weren't the words I had intended to say. And when they came out I thought, *Oh, no, that's too much for her. Sheila can't handle a challenge like that.*

I wanted to take the words back, but instead I waited. As she looked across the table at me, her eyes seemed to tell me that I had asked her to take on the world. When she didn't say a word, I was convinced I had asked too much of her. Doubt crossed my mind and told me that this was not going to be good for her.

After we talked about the challenge and how she felt, she said, "I'll do it, even though it will be very hard. I'm not sure I'll be able to follow through with it because it means facing a fear I've had for years. But I'll try."

Even after our session, I wondered if I had pushed her into an area that might hurt her. All I could think about was, "What if . . . ?"

At our next session, Sheila was excited. She had fulfilled the challenge and couldn't get over how much of an impact it had had on her. But what really impressed her was what her action meant to the other person involved. Facing her fear and accepting the challenge, as hard as it was, made all the difference. She then told me how she planned to take the challenge further.

For me, the impact on my mentee was another reminder to trust my God-given intuition. I learned that, though I need to be wise, I also need to make sure I don't make decisions for my mentees. After all, I wouldn't want someone to screen what she thought I could or could not handle.

When you give a challenge, allow your mentee to counter with what she thinks she can do. For example, if you have a mentee who is trying to overcome her fear of talking with people, you may challenge her to talk to ten people in the coming week. However, she may think she only has the confidence to talk with two. She needs to be able to voice her concern. After all, she's the one having to fulfill the challenge.

That said, you may think that talking with two people isn't much of a stretch. As her mentor, you need to help her see what she is capable of. Yes, maybe ten is too many but two may be too few, so negotiate and come to an agreement of what will move her out of her comfort zone and build her confidence.

What would happen if we thought less about how something we say affects us and more about the impact it has on others? What difference would it make if we replaced our need to have all the answers with the ability to leave a query, or make a request, or give a challenge?

## Mentoring Moment

1. Has what you've been learning in this book simply given you more knowledge or are you putting it into action? What action do you need to take today that will stretch you?

2. When you're in your next conversation with a friend or mentee, try leaving him or her with a query that's relevant to what you've been talking about. Follow-up the next week to find out what he or she discovered.

3. Read Luke 9:12-17. What request did Jesus make of the disciples? What did they learn about limitations and the power of God?

4. Read Luke 18:18-24. What challenge did Jesus give the rich, young ruler? Contrast his response with the response of the man in Luke 5:27-29.

# CHAPTER 15

# Cheering from the Sidelines

*A lot of people have gone further than they thought they could because someone else thought they could.*

—Author Unknown

BEFORE OUR CHILDREN were born, Jim and I went hiking every Saturday with a friend whom we had taken under our wing. On one of those hikes, we came to a roaring waterfall and a gorge that was forty-five-feet deep. Fortunately, a tree which was seventy-five-feet long and eight feet in diameter had fallen across the gorge, making a convenient natural bridge. Over time, the log had lost most of its bark and branches and shimmered in the constant spray from the waterfall. Smart or not, we decided to cross the wet log to the other side.

Jim easily made it over the slippery log and I followed behind, not daring to look at the rushing water below. Safe on solid ground, we both turned to watch our friend. Everything was going fine until Liz got halfway across and stopped. On her knees and hanging on to the wide log, she screamed, "I can't do this. I'm going back."

No amount of coaxing convinced her that it was the same distance to keep coming toward us as it was to turn around and go back. She looked as if she were frozen to the spot.

As the water swirled below and the waterfall spray showered us all, Jim yelled, "Liz, look at me. Don't look anywhere else except at me."

Lowering his voice but speaking loudly enough for her to hear, he continued. "Liz, listen. Of all the hikes we've been on together, have I ever taken you anywhere you couldn't handle?"

"N-n-n-o-o. But I'm scared."

After a few minutes of trying to persuade Liz to continue crawling along the log, and to keep her eyes forward rather than on the roaring water below, Jim assured her, "Liz, I know you can do this. You made it this far. Now you just have to come a little further. You can do it."

"But I don't know if I can go the rest of the way," she cried.

"Okay, how about if I meet you part way and crawl back with you?"

"No. Come all the way," she yelled.

"Okay. I'll come to you but I want you to start crawling toward me. Okay?"

"Okay," Liz stammered.

Jim continued to talk to Liz, while he inched toward her. Once he reached the place where she had become frozen in fear, he offered a few more encouraging words and turned on the log to face the direction from which he came. Together they made their way to safety.

Whether through formal or informal mentoring relationships, our mentees, as well as our family, friends, and peers, benefit when we cheer them on. Like Liz, they grow in confidence when we affirm and champion them. However, the truth is, we all need it from time to time.

Think about the last time someone championed or affirmed you. What did it do for you? How did it make you feel? Were you more confident and willing to open up to that person? Did it make you feel safe with him or her?

In a world where we are judged on our performance, or our looks, or our ability to do this or that, we need people in our lives who will affirm and champion us—not judge us. And, surprisingly, the people who appear to need encouragement the least may actually be the ones who need it the most.

As a mentor, your mentee will benefit greatly when you affirm him. He will grow in confidence when he knows you are standing on the sidelines as his champion. And he will detect if you are not being sincere or real.

## Affirm Your Mentee

Affirmation is not about making others feel good with flowery words or false accolades. It's about acknowledging their inner character, who they are and who they are becoming. It's about highlighting the inner strengths and qualities that God put within them.

Affirming someone goes to the heart of who she is and where she's growing. For some of us, it's difficult to receive an affirmation because we've rarely been given one and haven't learned how to receive it. Then there are those of us who think it's not spiritual to be acknowledged for something we did well, so we deflect any praise toward someone else. There are even those who hesitate to affirm someone because we're afraid he or she will become too proud.

The reality is that giving and receiving affirmation builds confidence and empowers us to keep going, which is what happens to your mentee when you acknowledge her. When you affirm your mentee, you will be able to tell whether or not the message hit home. You will see the impact on her face and in her body language. You will be able to watch her reaction and celebrate with her.

When I encouraged my friend Sharon to be true to herself and stand for a truth that was important to her, it was a giant step. Imagine the impact when she heard, "Sharon, you showed real courage when you took a stand for truth. That wasn't easy. You've come a long way in being bold to speak out for what you believe." Later, when she had second thoughts about whether or not she had done the right thing, her faith and confidence wavered. But it was the affirmation she had received that won out.

## Champion Your Mentee

When our children act in a way that is contrary to our morals or beliefs, or contrary to what we taught them, the frustration we feel in the present can overshadow all the positives of a lifetime. It becomes difficult to feel affirming. Yet it's in those times that our children most need someone to champion them. And if they aren't championed by us they will find it wherever they can.

A good friend of Donna's and mine has experienced how difficult it is to cheer from the sidelines. She would say that her life as a mother of teenagers has brought the best and the worst out in her. Yet, through it all, we have watched her grow as she learned to champion her teens, even when it was hard to find anything to champion them about. She has also opened her home to her children's friends, informally mentoring them in areas they don't see modeled in their own homes. Together they've baked cookies, shared meals, listened to music, and talked about what was important to them.

When we open the door of our home and invite people in, we are, in essence, saying that we accept them, which is similar to what happens when we mentor. People want to know that we accept them—their limitations, their fears, and their brilliance.

They want to know that we will be compassionate with them but that we will also ask them to be responsible for their actions and commitments. They want to know that we won't accept self-ridiculing or false condemnation that contradicts God's image of who they are.

As mentors, one of our roles is to be a champion. We support our mentees and cheer them on. We stand in their corner. We believe in them even when they doubt themselves.

Unlike affirming, which is about identifying qualities within a mentee, championing is about being a cheerleader. There will be times when your mentee feels incapable, weak, or tired. It's then that your role as champion is crucial. She needs to know that you're with her one hundred percent and that you believe in her. She needs to hear you say, "You've done this before. I know you can do it again. You are so good at this."

## Go the Extra Mile

In the earlier story about my friend Liz, we saw that cheering from the sidelines isn't always enough. Sometimes we need to retrace the steps we made in the mentoring relationship. Sometimes we need to go back to cheer our mentees on and give them that extra support as we encourage and assure them that we know they can do it.

Think about the last time you did something difficult and someone acknowledged you with an affirmation that underlined who you were in that situation. Now remember what it was like to receive it? Maybe it's time to take a step toward someone in your life and affirm him. Maybe he needs you as his champion. When you champion others, watch the difference it makes in their lives. And look for the difference it makes in yours.

## Mentoring Moment

1. Get together with a friend and share stories about someone who has championed each of you and the difference it made in your life.

2. Think about three people in your life and write a short sentence or two that affirms each of them. If you like, you may choose to get together with each one and share what you've written.

3. When I think of champions from biblical and secular history, I think of people like Barnabas, who championed Paul (Acts 9:26-27), and Anne Sullivan who championed Helen Keller. What other characters would you identify as true champions?

# SECTION V

## The Imprint of Mentoring

# CHAPTER 16

# Leaving a Lasting Legacy

*If you want to go fast, go alone. If you want to go far,*
*go together.*

—African proverb

A S A YOUNG girl, I dreamed of making a mark on the world.
I read the adventures of Danny Orlis, the Hardy Boys, and
Nancy Drew, who didn't bend to peer pressure or leave a
stone unturned in their quest to solve a mystery. I read biographies
of people like Anne Frank, David Livingstone, Gladys Aylward,
and Corrie ten Boom, who bravely faced challenges and sacrificed
themselves for others. And I felt a connection with everyday people
who demonstrated strength and creativity.

When I turned twenty-nine, I thought time was running out
for me and for the mark I wanted to leave. I remember saying, "I
haven't done a thing with my life. All I've accomplished is to put
my husband through university and have two children."

I adore my children and I'm happy to have helped Jim get
his degree, but at the time, it didn't feel like I'd done anything of
significance. Even when I later got involved in leading women

and working in the business world, I didn't think I was making a difference. Something I couldn't explain drove me to feel that there had to be more.

Over time I began to believe that maybe my mark would be the influence I had on the lives of my children. It was at that stage in my life that I prayed, "Lord, if the difference I'm supposed to make is found in my children and their children, then help me leave the best mark I can. You know my heart and my desire so I trust You to show me more when it's time. If there is more."

> *For I know the plans I have for you, declares the LORD, plans to prosper you and not to harm you, plans to give you hope and a future.*
>
> —Jer. 29:11, NIV

> *The Lord will fulfill His purpose for me.*
>
> —Ps 138:8

During the early stages of writing this book, my son called to say he had been tucking his daughter, Calista, into bed for the night when she said, "Daddy, I want to be just like Grandma."

I was speechless. Here was my then seven-year-old grand-daughter saying that she wanted to be just like me.

No, no, I thought, if she really knew everything about me she wouldn't say that. What if I disappoint her? What if she finds out that I make mistakes—that I'm not perfect?

I felt overwhelmed at the implied responsibility. Like Calista, I had always yearned to be like my grandma who was determined and courageous, encouraging and challenging, bold and unapologetic in being the woman God had created her to be. But now that I was a grandma, and hearing what it really meant, I felt waves of pride and apprehension, all wrapped up into one emotional bundle.

When I think of my passion to mobilize leaders to impact generations, I believe it's only possible when God is in it. He knows my weaknesses and failures, yet He trusts me to fulfill what He created me for. But when I look at my family through the lens of that same mission, the responsibility takes my breath away.

As I look at my grandchildren, I see four bright young people with blossoming leadership qualities born into them. And I am humbled to think that God handpicked me to be their grandma. I am the same woman He sees as perfect, even in my imperfection. And He chose me. What a tremendous responsibility. What a miraculous privilege.

Maybe you feel that way too.

*For it is God who is at work in you, both to will and to work for His good pleasure.*

—Phil. 2:13, NASB

## The Role of Surrender

Everything we've explored in this book is intended to challenge us to step up and make a difference and to enfold and engage others in healthy relationships that encourage and empower personal growth and a vibrant relationship with God. It's meant to show us how we affect other people and help us see that mentoring is about ordinary people learning and growing together.

The truth is that regardless of age, culture, or gender we all mentor every day. As we surrender our will to God, He is free to transform our lives, day by day, and use us to mentor others along the way.

In her book, *Between Women of God,* Donna Otto says something that I believe extends to men as well, "Ministry happens between women [and men] of God not because older women [or men] have crossed some spiritual finish line, but because they are being touched by the Lord's transforming power day by day."[17]

*Teach the older men to exercise self-control, to be worthy of respect, and to live wisely. They must have sound faith and be filled with love and patience. Similarly, teach the older women to live in a way that honors God. They must not slander others or be heavy drinkers. Instead, they should teach others what is good. These older women must train the younger women to love their husbands and their children, to live wisely and be pure, to work in their homes, to do good, and to be submissive to their husbands. Then they will not bring shame on the word of God. In the same way, encourage the young men to live wisely. And you yourself must be an example to them by doing good works of every kind. Let everything you do reflect the integrity and seriousness of your teaching.*

—Titus 2:2-7, NLT

Imagine the mark we would leave if we surrendered our past and present pain, joy, sadness, and dreams to the One who already knows all about them and who has been crying or rejoicing right along with us. Imagine the difference we would make if, instead of running away *from* God, we each ran *to* God.

No matter how many years we've been on this earth or how much time we have left, we can leave a God-honoring mark and make a kingdom difference when we begin by saying, "Okay, Lord, here's my life, past, present, and future, good, bad, and ugly. I surrender it all to You. Now, who do You want me to encourage or walk beside for a while?"

## One More Fingerprint in Endless Time

The impact and legacy of mentoring is about what we leave for tomorrow, but it starts today. Mentoring takes the lessons we've learned in our own journeys and passes them on to the next generations. It never gives up. It walks alongside others, nurturing their hearts for God. It's about how we live and the interest we take in others. It's about taking time to pour ourselves into another life regardless of what generation that person represents. It's about living as Christ would and doing what He asks of us each day.

We may start our life journey with great intentions that don't work out the way we intended. And yes, we may have ups and downs along the way, but God uses every struggle and victory to bring glory to Himself and to make a difference for eternity. It's what we do in the struggles and the victories that make the difference. It's that difference that we pass on.

Freda is a humble, quiet woman with a heart for children and a soul for serving others. A number of years ago, she and her ailing dad moved into a house with a neighborhood full of children. As Freda worked in her yard, the children came to see what she was doing and, in Freda's words, "We became friends. They would come over to talk, bake cookies, and play pool or other games."

When Freda's dad died, the opportunity came to offer her home to host a backyard, five-day Bible club taught by *Child Evangelism Fellowship* workers. From the friendships she and the children had already established, the club became a hub of activity. During the final year in her home, Freda taught the club herself and, although she is now retired and living in a senior's complex, the club continues. It just looks different.

The children, who grew to love and respect Freda, followed her. In order to spend quality time with each one, she divided the group by age. Five children, ages nine and ten, meet with her every second Thursday. Two girls, ages 13 and 14, come by to spend time on alternate Thursdays. And two boys, ages 12 and 13, visit every second Tuesday. During their times together, they talk, bake, play games, and do a Bible lesson.

On Sunday when I see Freda come into church and sit with children on either side of her, I can't help but think that she is a walking example of lifestyle mentoring. She may not consider herself a mentor, but as she pours herself into the lives of young people by being available to talk, bake cookies, play games, or bring them to church, she is leaving a mentor's fingerprint.

Freda has influenced many children to whom she has been a shelter from the turmoil of their broken or hurting lives. And, along the way, she has affected their parents as well. Who knows what mark each of these lives will leave on the world, all because a single woman made herself available?

Like Freda, we don't know whom we might be mentoring. One of our mentees could become the next doctor or scientist to develop a cure for a worldwide disease. Or the next prime minister or president of a great country. Or the next Christian leader to change the direction of a nation. He or she may be like some of the people Donna and I were with when we recently went to Trinidad with a team of women on a short-term missions trip.

During that trip we were privileged to attend the fortieth anniversary celebrations of a church that Donna and Edith Johnson, her then ministry partner, had begun in a village called Marabella. The full story of their adventure and the miracles God performed in the planting of that church are part of *Trinidad: My Home, My People*, a biography about Edith who, after more than fifty years, still ministers in Trinidad.[18]

In the early days of the church, Donna and Edith began working with teenagers who were curious about the two white women who weren't afraid to live and work like the rest of the people in the village. Forty years later, many of the original twenty-five or thirty young people traveled from many parts of the world to praise God for His faithfulness and to pay tribute to the two women whom God used to bring them the gospel.

Today, almost all of those young people, who are now adults with children and grandchildren, are in full-time ministry as pastors, educators, missionaries, youth workers, church leaders, and

Bible teachers all over the world. From the early example of two missionary women who mentored them, they in turn mentored the next generation who are now influencing yet another generation. Beginning with Edith and Donna, that's four generations. Each individual added his or her fingerprint to the marks that were first left by two single, obedient women of God.

The next time you see a ripple in a lake or hear the sound of streams melding together to form a river of rushing water, let those sights and sounds remind you of mentoring. Because, in a similar way, as we mentor someone near us, the effects reach far beyond that one person. It affects our life, that person's life, and many other people in their life whom we may never know.

Each mark we make is part of eternity, and the legacy we leave is one more fingerprint in endless time.

## The Gift

In dark comfort and slumber
I was formed in peace
Till it was thrust upon me
From ooze of night
Into bright reality
I was born.
I never asked for it
Never knew what it was
Confused at first
Bewildered
What to do with it?
This gift of short duration
Consume it?
Squander it?
Share it?
Offer it?

Till I realized, one day
I will be asked,
"What did you do with it?
What profit did you bring?
What legacy was made?
How'd it honor the King?"
This life given me as a gift
One day will be given back.
What will my answer be, then?

—Jim Griffiths
©Used by permission

## Mentoring Moment

1.  What difference has *A Mentor's Fingerprint* made in your life?

2.  What mark are you leaving on the world?

3.  What difference are you making in the lives of people around you?

4.  What step are you prepared to take today to make a difference for tomorrow?

# Endnotes

## Chapter 3

1. http://www.realtor.org/eomag.nsf.
2. http://barefootcreative.com/res/pdf/bf_youth_study.pdf.

## Chapter 4

3. Donna Otto, *Between Women of God* (Eugene, Oregon: Harvest House Publishers, 1995), 52.
4. http://mentoring-works.com/definitions_of_mentoring.html
5. http://en.wikipedia.org/wiki/Mentor.
6. Paul D. Stanley and J. Robert Clinton, *Connecting: The Mentoring Relationships You Need to Succeed in Life* (Colorado Springs, Colorado: NavPress, 1992), 42.

## Chapter 5

7. Carson Pue, *Mentoring Leaders* (Grand Rapids, MI: Baker Books, 2005), 258.

## Chapter 8

8. Donna Otto, *Between Women of God* (Eugene, Oregon: Harvest House Publishers, 1995), 147.
9. Andrew Murray, *Abide in Christ* (New York: Grosset & Dunlap Publishers), 12.
10. Ibid, 13.
11. Hudson T. Armerding, *Leadership* (Wheaton, IL: Tyndale, 1978).

## Chapter 9

12. Dallas Willard, *The Spirit of the Disciplines* (New York: HarperCollins Publishers, 1991), ix.
13. John Ortberg, *The Life You've Always Wanted* (Grand Rapids, Michigan: Zondervan, 2002), 182-191.

## Chapter 11

14. www.thecoaches.com.
15. Laura Whitworth, Henry Kimsey-House & Phil Sandahl, *Co-Active Coaching* (Palo Alto, California: Davies-Black Publishing, 1998), 34-39.

## Chapter 12

16. Dietrich Bonheoffer, *Life Together* (New York: Harper & Row Publishers, Inc., 1954).

## Chapter 16

17. Donna Otto, *Between Women of God* (Eugene, Oregon: Harvest House Publishers, 1995), 147.
18. Max Inglis, *Trinidad: My Home, My People.* (Port Colborne, ON: Gospel Folio Press, 2009).

For additional resources or to have Ann and/or Donna speak at your next event, visit

www.fingerprintministries.com

Ann and Donna are honored to hear from their readers. If you wish to write to them please email them directly at:

ann@fingerprintministries.com

OR

donna@fingerprintministries.com